The Power To Effect CHANGE

The Power To Effect CHANGE

Pastor Gary W. Carter

Drayton Valley Word of Life Centre

Endorsement

The Power to Effect Change is a manual of practical principles that will help church leaders in their search for answers to community transformation.

Gary Carter is a strategic thinker, church planter and communicator. He has applied "present day truths" in his personal life, church and community, effecting great change.

The Power to Effect Change is a manual born out of Gary's own experience and relationship with God as he has developed intercessors, trained leaders and developed a strong relationship with his community.

The principles presented in **The Power to Effect Change** can be easily applied to your community with the same results.

Mel C. Mullen
Pastor – Word of Life Centre
Red Deer, Alberta
Canada

Dedication

Dedicated **to my wife and family** who lived through the life experiences we had in order to learn these principles.

And to our church.......

.......*The greatest team I know!*

Thank-you!

Contents

Foreword

Pastor Gary Carter is serious about changing his city. While many talk about effecting transformation, few are actually "hitting the mark." The principles in **The Power to Effect Change** are tried and proven.

Pastor Carter's book gives the reader keys to team building for city transformation. City changing doesn't need to be a mystery! The proof of the application of this book is in the community of Drayton Valley. Drayton Valley's citizens have been impacted through the prayer and love of Drayton Valley Word of Life Centre. They even petitioned the town council to establish a bylaw prohibiting the operation of any public place that features adult entertainment!

For those searching for answers on how apostles, prophets, and intercessors should work together—this book is for you! It is not simply theory. It works.

Cindy Jacobs
Co-founder
Generals of Intercession
Colorado Springs, Colorado

Introduction

I am writing this book as a testimony of what we have seen happen in our town of Drayton Valley.

Years ago, I saw a passage of scripture in the book of Acts that caused me to begin asking the Lord to show His presence in an unmistakable way.

> ***...to whom He also presented Himself alive after His suffering by many <u>infallible proofs</u>, being seen by them during forty days and speaking of the things pertaining to the kingdom of God.***
>
> ***Acts 1:3***

Our leadership and prayer teams asked the Lord to reveal Himself and His desires in a way that His presence in our city would be obvious to us all. We also wanted Him to show us the principles that we needed to use to **"Pastor our city"** and see it transformed for the glory of God. We asked Him to show us in such a way that we could clearly document the process, and even more importantly, that He would show us in a way that we could reproduce anywhere in the world.

I believe He has answered our prayers!

The Blacksmiths of God!

Now there was no blacksmith to be found throughout all the land of Israel, for the Philistines said, "Lest the Hebrews make swords or spears." But all the Israelites would go down to the Philistines to sharpen each man's plowshare, his mattock, his ax, and his sickle; and the charge for a sharpening was a pim for the plowshares, the mattocks, the forks, and the axes, and to set the points of the goads. So it came about, on the day of battle, that there was neither sword nor spear found in the hand of any of the people who were with Saul and Jonathan. But they were found with Saul and Jonathan his son. And the garrison of the Philistines went out to the pass of Michmash.

1 Samuel 13:19-23

We saw a principle in this passage of scripture that revealed a spiritual warfare strategy of the enemy.

One of his goals since the early church is to remove the spiritual blacksmiths from the body of Christ. Blacksmiths are people who are able to sharpen the weapons, build new ones when needed, or repair the ones already in use in the battle. They have the skill to envision the finished product, turn up the heat, pound things out and keep the cutting edge in every weapon of warfare. When we lose the blacksmiths our weapons get blunt edges that, although they may cause some harm to the enemy, don't have the cutting-edge sharpness to really penetrate.

The blacksmiths I see in the body are people with Apostolic giftings. They have the ability to see what needs to be repaired, built or refined to win the war. We need these people in all of our ministries and in every sector of our cities.

We can see this kind of gifting in action throughout our society. Not all of them are Pastors or Evangelists—some are business people, some are politicians, some are housewives and blue collar workers, but they all have the special qualities working in them that makes them what I call the blacksmiths of our cities or nation. These are the type of people I like to work with!

Blacksmiths have some common characteristics :

1. they have a long-term vision for the community,

2. they believe in teamwork, and

3. they have the leadership skills to build teams to accomplish the tasks.

The Lord has established the heavenlies in such a way that forces us to work in unity and one accord if we want to see the fullness of His glory. I call this the "corporate anointing." (There will be more about this in a later chapter.)

I was going to call this book **"The Systematic Sovereignty of God"** because I see that in every area of life the Lord is sovereign, but at the same time He has some very repetitive systems. Salvation is one of these systems. He works sovereignly in people's lives but the system or requirements of salvation stays the same. Prosperity or any other blessing found in God's Word can be described as a system in which we have our part to play, and if we do our part, God will do His sovereign work on our behalf. In the last six years we have found that the Lord has a plan for every city, but something has gone wrong to get it off track. He is waiting for people of vision and determination to identify and fulfill His plan.

In this book I am giving you the keys we have used here in our community. I believe these principles will give you the *"Power to Effect Change!"*

Pastor your city!

If there is one thing I can influence you to do in this book it would be this, "Pastor your city, not just your church."

If we are doing a good job Pastoring our community, our churches will grow as a by-product of that effort. We are not a fortress in an enemy's land where we can simply raise the drawbridge whenever we feel threatened. We, the church, are the invading force! We are the ones that are invading the enemy's strongholds! I see the born-again church as an army of the Lord and we are on the attack. We are moving through the enemy's land seeking out the areas where he has established strongholds. It's his fortress we are identifying. It's his drawbridge that is going up. It's he who will be going into hiding, because the church of Jesus Christ is on the move!

Many of us in the body of Christ seem to think that we are standing still and that there are wave after wave of attacks coming against us. This gives us a victim mentality. Well, I say the reality is that it's the other way around! We are going forward like a boat going through water and we are hitting the waves of resistance with enough force and break- through power to get to the other side! It's we who are on the move!

Any time a church stops going forward, the battle stops. We can still have a sensation of movement as we go up and down on the waves, but we aren't going forward anymore. When this happens we are driven in the directions the waves send us, rather than driving our way to the place we want to be. So I would say to you today, if you are feeling the waves of attack...good! It's you that's going forward! It's you that's breaking through! Don't give the devil the credit—he's not the one on the move—you are! Keep going!

If you feel like you are going through hell, I have some counsel for you...DON'T STOP! This is not the place you want to set up camp and stay for awhile! Set your eyes on the vision God gave you that started you on your journey in the first place and keep walking until you get to the other side!

That's why I say that you need to Pastor and lead your city, not just your church. I started to do this ten years ago and I have seen our church grow as fast as we are able to handle it, and we don't do crusades or outreaches or any other approach to winning souls. This is very ironic in that I'm an evangelist by nature. I'm not against doing outreaches (I like them), but I just haven't had time to do one. We just found out what work the Father had called us to do in the community and put our energy into doing it.

I'm not writing this book to establish new theology or to challenge yours. I am writing it as a testimony of what we did and what we have seen the Lord do with it, in the hopes that you may be able to apply some of these principles and experience the blessing we have here. I believe that every Pastor is called to be an elder of his city. There are also key elders (business, political, etc.) or key Pastors that are to lead with what I call an Apostolic leadership.

There are many ways the word "apostolic" is being used today—some I like, some I don't—so please allow me to clarify what I mean by using that word.

What is a Modern Day Apostle?

This word has been used by non-denominational churches for the most part, but I see the same leadership style and ability functioning in almost all of the denominations in our cities. So I don't believe it's a new approach at all, it is only getting new attention as a leadership style today. I would even go as far as to say we are returning to the most Biblical leadership structure.

> *Now you are the body of Christ, and members individually. And God has appointed these in the church: <u>first apostles,</u> second prophets, third teachers, after that miracles, then gifts of healings, helps, administrations, varieties of tongues.*
>
> **1 Corinthians 12:27-28**

What I mean by the term Apostle is this:

1. **Leadership that is larger than self.** This type of leader has a vision that demands teamwork to

carry it out. If they can't build a team they can't accomplish the task. They think about the city, or the nation or even international issues and don't have to be asked to jump into the middle of the problems.

2. **They thrive on problems** (especially if they aren't self-generated). For the most part, these leaders think and respond better under pressure than they do when things are going good. Still waters, long green grass and sunny days don't interest them much. Give them rapids, stink weeds and thunderstorms and they will think they have just gone to heaven. (It may sound weird, but if you are one or know one well, you will know what I'm talking about.)

3. **They have a fathering heart towards the people.** Pastors have a natural tendency to want to comfort or set up camp with you when life has driven you into the cave, but that doesn't describe an apostolic leader. A person (male or female) with the Apostolic giftings working in his/her life will usually only have idle conversation with you in that place. When the challenge begins, like a father or mother, the Apostle ensures that the instructions of life are given and the marching orders are proclaimed as they grab the burdens you carry and charge the mountains of life. They really do believe that if you will follow, you will win! (I have to admit it does have impressive results.)

4. **They are the ones who have faith for you when you don't.** They can see what is lacking in your

life, your thinking or your actions, and inspire you to rise to a new level in every way. They can see past your circumstances to the finished product and the will of the Lord in your situation so they can give you the shortest route and safest path to travel. They see the solutions to troubles that everyone else seems to miss.

5. **They have a great ability to inspire confidence in others.** They are able to bring out the best that God has placed deep in the hearts of all of us, even things that we didn't even realize were there.

6. **They are gifted in vision** with an ability to analyze the reality of the present and determine the ultimate goals as they lay out the easy steps for us to get from where we are to where God has called us to be.

Many of these leaders seem larger than life. They talk like they can do anything. They can even come across as prideful or have the appearance of being controlling. But, in fact, any that I have met are quite the opposite. Their whole joy and purpose in life is to watch their spiritual sons and daughters rise higher and go farther than they have ever been! I have met many of them. They are in every city of every nation. They are in the government, the church, the business community, the school systems, or any other place you will find people. They are there, they are male and female, and if you are one...I thank God for you and your gifting.

The "Power to Effect Change!"

The Bible says that we are to be the head and not the tail, above and not below! One day we will give an account to God that goes beyond how big of a church we built, or how many conferences we preached at. I believe we will give an account of **how we Pastored the city He gave us.**

I don't believe that the responsibility before God for the future of our cities is in the office of the Mayor or the city government. I don't believe we will be able to say "We just obeyed the lawmakers or the school system," or to say "that's what the majority wanted." We serve the Lord of a kingdom, not a democracy. We are the ones, as the Pastors and elders of our city, that God will hold accountable for what **we allow man to accept as normal.** We have allowed the law of the land to become our gauge of morals and ethics. The law was never intended to be the gauge. The law was put in place to say "if you get this low in your morals and ethics we are going to punish you!" The world needs a value system that is above the mandated law of the land. We, the church, have the responsibility before God to proclaim, to teach and to establish by example a higher level for the world to follow.

The devil gets to have his way only if the only other force on the face of the earth lets him. That's us! The church! The Body of Christ. We have the power and authority not only to merely want change or pray for change, we have the authority **to command change** in the heavenlies. God has given to us, the corporate church, the "**Power to effect change!**"

So God knows we have it, and the devils certainly know we do, but it's we who haven't grasped the reality of who we are and what we can do!

It was a passage of scripture that changed my thinking.

> **Asa...<u>commanded Judah</u> to seek the LORD God of their fathers, and to observe the law and the commandment.**
>
> **2 Chronicles 14:4**

I caught myself thinking, "Wouldn't it be nice to have the ability to command people to serve God and to have them respond?" I know it doesn't work that way in the natural world, but it did inspire a thought in me. **We do have the authority in the spirit realm to command what we want to see!**

The body of Christ has the corporate power *to bring the spiritual climate of our city into order with the purposes of God.*

Job 22:28 says:

> **You will also declare a thing, And it will be**

established for you; So light will shine on your ways.

We have the power already in the corporate body of Christ to bring change to our city. Life and death are in the power of the tongue, and when the body of Christ rises up with one voice and one sound the glory of the Lord falls!

There isn't any one superstar ministry or church that is taking their city alone. The Lord has designed a system that requires us to live up to the principles in Acts 1 of unity, prayer, fellowship, and one accord if we ever want to experience an Acts 2 city-changing reality of God.

Windows and doors of relationship and communication!

Every church in a city has a part of the revelation and a part of the gifting for transformation. We sang a song for years that had the words "let the walls fall down." This is a great thought as well as a great principle of unity, but in actual fact, *nobody wants to live with his neighbor!* It doesn't matter how nice my neighbor is, what good friends we are or what common interests we may have. I still don't want to tear down the walls of my home and join it to his. I want my own identity. I want a place that allows me to be what I want to be and do what I want to do without having to accommodate other interests or likes. This is the same in the spiritual world. We really don't want to all become alike. We don't want to move into the same house and all be the same. I like all of the variety in the kingdom of God and I think it's been His plan all along. I do, however, want to have relationship with my neighbors.

I asked our intercessory prayer teams to address this issue and they came back to me and said, **"Pastor, don't try to tear down the walls, just put some windows and doorways in them!"**

What a great thought! (Pastors, if you don't have functioning and successful prayer teams in your church, make it the top priority to build and train some—they have been the key to our success!)

These windows and doors are made up of relationship and communication!

I don't want to move in with my neighbor, but I do want to have a window so I can see him and wave at him when he's there. I do want to have open doors of relationship so we can invite each other in for fellowship and help whenever needed!

When I have relationship and communication with my neighbors (other churches), I start to see, hear and appreciate what God is saying to them.

In any city there are many churches. Every church has a piece of the revelation of God and the gifts to carry it out. You can only go forward in your ministry (locally, nationally or internationally) based on the revelation and gifting that God has given you. Other churches and ministries have been established by God in your city (or nations) that also have a piece of the revelation of His plans and purposes, as well as the gifts to carry them out. The more we work together the more pieces of revelation we can put on the table. It's like a puzzle, and as soon as enough of the pieces are revealed, we can get a clearer picture of the full purposes of God.

This reveals:

1. The redemptive purpose or the reason your church or city exists in the first place.

2. The violations against God's purposes that stops it from coming to pass.

3. The anchor points and strategies of the devil.

4. Your strengths and strategies for your city.

The goal isn't for us all to become alike in our theology or our presentation. **The goal is rather to embrace our differences,** determine the reason why our churches exist and work together by adding our purpose and gifting to other churches in the city to accomplish a common goal.

The goal is always to bring an atmosphere of God to our community so the minds of men can be freed from the lies and influence of the devil and opened to the things of God.

I want to break down the three key elements of transformation as we go through this process.

The first element I want to cover in the next chapter is "**Jurisdictional authority.**"

I feel I should clarify what I mean by the word 'authority.' Many are afraid to use this word today. There has been a lot of abuse of authority as well as a lot of teaching about independence and freedom, which says I don't need to be accountable to anyone else. The authority I am speaking about is having authority or ruling power to effect change in the spirit realm. You can't dictate authority over people. You can only use influence and wise counsel. But there is another spiritual truth; you can't counsel a devil—it takes spiritual jurisdictional authority to deal with them!

There is an authority from God placed on our "Redemptive Purpose." This gives us whatever breakthrough abilities we need to accomplish the God-ordained purpose He has given us. I also believe that it has a regional nature to it as well. I believe there are city Apostles, provincial or state Apostles, national Apostles and those for various regions or people groups of the world.

I see the structure as being like the original Jerusalem council. In this structure, each one has input and wisdom based on his or her sphere of influence, defined by people group or geographical location. When an Apostolic ministry is in their region or sphere of influence they can function by authority in the spirit realm. When they speak the principles of God it brings a measurable change to the natural world! When they are outside of their sphere or region of jurisdictional authority they function by influence. They have great ability to influence those that have jurisdictional authority in another region, but they themselves don't have the same measurable power to effect change in that region or sphere.

Jurisdictional authority can be broken down into three elements:

Key #1 – Redemptive Purpose
Key #2 – Personal Spiritual Supremacy
Key #3 – The Corporate Anointing

Key #1—
Redemptive Purpose

In this section I want to present one of the greatest city-transformation principles the Lord has taught us.

In Jeremiah chapter 1 we see that God said to Jeremiah;

> **"Before I formed you in the womb I knew you; Before you were born I sanctified you; I ordained you a prophet to the nations."**
>
> **Jeremiah 1:5**

This shows me that before we are born there is a God-inspired and planned reason for each one of us to exist. God has a plan and purpose for our lives and He has put everything we need within us to carry it out.

I call this our "Redemptive Purpose," or the reason we were created in the first place.

If we were born into a perfect world and kept our

eyes on the Lord as we followed His plan, we would walk with God all the days of our lives. But we are born into a sinful world with a sinful nature, and we make choices in life that get us off track from His original redemptive purpose. When we get saved (accept Jesus Christ as our personal Savior) we are redeemed by the blood of the Lamb. This doesn't refer only to being spared from the judgement we really deserve from God. It also means we get restored back to the original plan He had for us in the first place before we were born and before we started to get off track. If we will allow Him to work in our lives, we can identify what He created us to do and be restored to that plan.

This principle can be applied to churches as well. If the Lord really started that church, He must have had a reason in mind even before it was born. He not only had a reason, but He put all the gifting in it to carry out His plans. The same can be said for a city or a nation. God had a reason for them to exist even before they were birthed. I don't believe that man chooses the boundaries of nations or where to build a city. *God has a plan in place and we can discover it!*

A person that doesn't know why he exists or what his purpose is will never feel a sense of peace and purpose in himself. He lacks hope, and no matter how successful he is in life he can't feel fulfilled. The same is true for a city or a nation. A city that doesn't know its purpose before God is a city of unrest, independence, strife and competition. Even more interesting to me is that about 75% of the Pastors I have ministered to all over the world don't know why their church exists or what God wanted to do when

He birthed it beyond doing the Sunday services, weddings and funerals. I believe that, as a church, we are to help every person that walks through our doors unlock the redemptive purpose and giftings that God has given them. As they do this, they can join a team of people of like faith to accomplish the tasks they are called to do.

Churches in a community that don't know what God created them for can't really set a definite direction, so they can't really lead. It's like the blind leading the blind!

In our cities we have churches that are doing the weddings and funerals and caring for the people that show up on Sundays, but who don't think about any greater purpose beyond these tasks. We can be task-oriented and busy but at the same time not really leading the community closer to the purposes of God.

Another community environment that can develop is when the churches each identify why they exist and start out on a journey to fulfill these purposes. The problem is, they can all be walking in their own redemptive giftings and purposes and yet still be going in different directions. This happens because they haven't defined the redemptive purpose (or the reason their city exits), which would give them a common target. Sooner or later, this creates an equal tension in the spirit realm and no one can seem to break through any further. The results are seen in church growth peaks. There are church growth cycles in any community that can be identified and traced historically. We can also see this in new church plants that explode in initial growth but eventually run into the same regional problem.

Community or national cycles that can be identified and traced are keys to finding the violations to our redemptive purpose for our cities and nation. These cycles also help us to know what to take before God so He can redeem or restore them to His original plan.

What we need to know is,

1. our redemptive purpose for our personal life,

2. the redemptive purpose for our church, and

3. how these connect to the redemptive purpose for our city and ultimately our nation, as well as our part to fulfill it.

We have had division in the body of Christ over doctrinal issues, sheep stealing fears and many other things, but when we identify our redemptive purpose, it allows us as individuals to be connected to the church of like purpose. It also allows us to relate to another church that may be theologically different, but has a particular skill and purpose before God that can partner with us to influence the city. When we identify the reason we all exist, we are then able to unite together with the vision, purpose and our part of the plan that God has for our city. I call this **"community alignment."**

It also gives us the ability to embrace other churches in our city because we have a real sense of needing their help and their part of the revelations to complete the fullness of what God wants done.

Have you noticed that churches and cities that are experiencing a move of God around the world seem to have very little or nothing in common with a move of the Spirit in another city. The doctrinal statements are not exactly the same. The methodology is different. The expressions and experiences are quite different, as well. So how can one God and one Spirit,be doing such different things in the same season of time? Why can't it be packaged and sold? Why is it hit and miss even to try and copy the philosophy and strategy? Why do exactly the same procedures, doctrines and programs bless one city, but blow churches apart in another city that tries the same things?

There are those that say, "I guess the Lord just chose to bless us!" **That's nice, but it's not theologically sound.** The Bible says...

> *Then Peter opened his mouth and said: "In truth I perceive that <u>God shows no partiality</u>."*
>
> ### Acts 10:34

When we think that the Lord randomly chooses those He wants to bless, it breeds thoughts of envy and jealousy. Also, we all have seen Pastors that appear to do all the wrong things but walk into blessings. Others spend their whole ministry life working hard, praying and living as pure as they can and still see very little fruit or city impact for their labors. We all have our excuses and ways to spiritualize them so we can convince ourselves we are winning, but inside all of us are discouragements and frustrations that we don't even like to think about.

The answer to all of these questions is the same! Because a ministry has fruit doesn't mean they have found increased favor with God or that they are more holy. *They have tapped into the redemptive purpose for their city even if they don't realize it.* They are doing the right kind of ministry needed in their region to correct the violations and fulfill the original purposes of God.

Here are some examples of what I mean:

A city that has a violation of pride would need a strong ministry of humility and repentance.

A city with a violation of lust would need a strong ministry of purity.

A city with greed, generosity.

A city with rebellion to God would need a ministry that is opposite, like intimacy or obedience.

Whatever the violation that caused a breach in the hedge of protection and allowed a spiritual stronghold to be legally established is corrected by ministry of opposite acts of correction.

5

The Hedge of Protection

This is another principle that it is important to note at this time.

> **Then the LORD said to Satan, "Have you considered My servant Job, that there is none like him on the earth, a blameless and upright man, one who fears God and shuns evil?" So Satan answered the LORD and said, "Does Job fear God for nothing? <u>"Have You not made a hedge around him, around his household, and around all that he has on every side</u>? You have blessed the work of his hands, and his possessions have increased in the land.**

> **Job 1:8-10**

Do you see what the devil is saying? God had placed a protection around Job, around his household and around all that he had! I believe that this is true for us all. As individuals with a specific call and purpose on our lives (we all have one, not just Pastors) *the hedge is there to protect us in it.*

It's the same for a church. Before it was birthed, God had a plan for it. With that plan came the anointing, the ability and the hedge of protection to walk it out. It applies equally to cities as well as nations.

The devil doesn't have any legal rights to establish a stronghold in an individual, a church, a city or a nation. **He has to have found a doorway!** In the church we hear "the devil is sure doing a work," but I say he doesn't have the right to do anything unless he can find a doorway. If the devil is working in the church, drive him out! You have the spiritual authority over him.

> *Behold, I give you the authority to trample on serpents and scorpions, and over all the power of the enemy, and nothing shall by any means hurt you.*
>
> *Luke 10:19*

We have the Name of Jesus, we have the anointing of the Holy Ghost, we have the power of praise, we have the precious blood of the Lamb, so the devil doesn't get any say! Take authority over him and shut him down!

The problem seems to be that we take authority over him but he doesn't go away. In fact, he can even get more active! Why? Because he has found a way to be there by violation or judgement.

Violations

The hedge of protection is there, and it is stronger

than any of the devil's devices. All he can do is to work on creating a doorway.

For where _envy and self-seeking_ exist, confusion and every evil thing are there.

James 3:16

He works on our carnal nature and gets us to disobey or violate a principle of God, and that opens the doorway of permission before God for him to come in. This isn't new. He has been doing it since the Garden of Eden.

I started to think about all the meetings I have attended in our country to bring reconciliation to people groups for past offences. I am in favor of the process and I rejoice that people are working at restoring relationships. I believe this is one step towards restoring a city or a nation back to its original purpose before God.

I thought about how long it would take us to apologize to every people group for every sin, and I knew by the time we did it for everyone, we would have offended or violated a whole new generation of people and would have to start over. So I let my mind wander through the process in fast reverse! I thought about the French-English conflict of our own country. Before this was the violation between the First Nations people and the original founders of the present land boundaries and government. I thought, then, that it must have started before Canada even became a nation, so I went further back to the older nations of Europe. Who was before them? Well, I guess it must have been the Holy Land where it all started. There are those who have taken it that far and have done identificational repentance to try to restore relationship harmony with these people groups. **I say, "Good for you!" I join with your intentions and applaud your efforts.**

I started to think, however, "Where was the first violation? Who was the first one?" I eventually backed it through the ages of time in reverse order and thought I had hit the target in the garden on Eden! It wasn't long before I realized there was a violation even before that one. It was a violation recorded in...

> *How you are fallen from heaven, O Lucifer, son of the morning! How you are cut down to the ground, You who weakened the nations! For you have said in your heart: 'I will ascend into heaven, I will exalt my throne above the stars of God; I will also sit on the mount of the congregation On the farthest sides of the north; I will ascend above the heights of the clouds, I will be like the Most High.'*
>
> *Isaiah 14:12-14*

The first violation was right in the throneroom! It was a violation of an attitude of pride. Lucifer didn't get demon possessed! There weren't any devils there! He just got an attitude of pride that caused him to disobey and rebel against God **in his heart!** It wasn't even in his actions or his words, it was an attitude of his heart! This in itself has a profound reality—God doesn't deal with our words or our actions, He deals with the issues of the heart! Right actions with wrong heart still won't please God!

Lucifer fell and became the adversary in the

Garden of Eden. There he met with man. The Bible doesn't say he possessed Adam and Eve. He didn't overtake them supernaturally. He started to mess with their minds. He got them to question God. He got them to question God's word. He got them to think that what he had to offer was better and that God had a wrong motive for telling them not to eat of the tree of knowledge of good and evil. As soon as they surrendered to that influence they opened themselves up to the devil and it gave him a doorway. **The second violation took place and carnality was birthed.**

James 3:16 in my words:

> *Through pride-based carnality every evil thing exists!*

This principle applies to people, churches, cities and nations!

Before you were born (individual, church, city, nation) God had a plan. He placed a hedge of protection around it. The devil started to develop a strategy against that plan but he didn't have any rights or power to resist God. So he influenced those that were being used by God to fulfill that purpose and messed with their thinking and stirred their pride, greed and selfishness until they violated the purposes of God. That violation created a legal doorway for the enemy to come in and establish a presence in the region.

One preacher I heard put it this way when he was referring to a regional presence or stronghold of the devil:

> *"When the people of a region accept or*

surrender to the devil's influence on their carnal nature, [it] develops mental attitudes driven by demonic forces"

I think that is well put!

Key #2—Personal Spiritual Supremacy

What do we do about the violations?

First, we need to identify them. This is what requires the work.

It starts with you, the Pastor or leader who has a call for your city. That call comes with the right vision, influence (with proven results that everyone can see) and the abilities to carry it out.

We tend to think that our strength will be the determining factor in taking a city for Jesus. We think the anointing and giftings God placed in our lives to carry out His will are the city-changing keys. However, the words of the Lord to the Apostle Paul give us a hint at another great truth.

> **And He said to me, "My grace is sufficient for you, for _My strength is made perfect in weakness_." Therefore most gladly I will rather boast in my infirmities, that the power of Christ may rest upon me.**
>
> **2 Corinthians 12:9**

I have found that it is equally important, if not even "more important" to identify and acknowledge our weaknesses. We put such great trust in our strengths since that's what we want everyone to see. But the Bible says the devil can't stop the anointing!

> **And it shall come to pass in that day, that his burden shall be taken away from off thy shoulder, and his yoke from off thy neck, and <u>the yoke shall be destroyed because of the anointing</u>.**
>
> **Isaiah 10:27**

He knows he can't resist you in the areas of your strength. The anointing breaks the yoke! Every time he tries to contain you in the area of your anointing or the gifts and abilities God has placed in you before you were born, it breaks through—it can't be contained. I call this ability our "Breakthrough Anointing!"

We all have it in us, but for each one it is different because it is relative to our individual redemptive purpose or the reason God has us on the earth in the first place.

When personal discouragement starts to overcome people with a prophetic gifting, they will find prophecy will bring a flooding presence of God into their spirits. With it comes a breakthrough power or ability we call 'anointing.' This flooding presence of God breaks the yoke and sets them free. It works well if you have a prophetic motivational gifting, but if you are an evangelist by nature, it may not bring that same flooding presence of God when you prophecy. Instead, you will find the flooding presence that releases a breakthrough anointing by going out and telling people about the gospel. I have found that even thinking about what we can and will do in the direction of our gifting brings that flooding presence of God into our spirits. For someone with an Apostolic ministry all they need to do is start to think about vision. As they move their minds out from the natural and into the realms of vision and strategy they will be flooded with a breakthrough anointing. This will break any heaviness, depression or any other yoke the devil is trying to place on them. The key thought is this: God has placed a supernatural breakthrough anointing upon your life. You need to identify what it is and exercise it daily so it will continually keep you from the yoke of the enemy.

The devil isn't stupid—he knows the Word and knows the power that Jesus has given us. So he looks for doorways of weakness! He looks for a weak area in your life, your words or your relationships and then tries to establish an open doorway through offence, pride or jealousy. He has hopes that you will surrender to it and cause a violation against the principles of God. This gives him legal rights to be there. The anointing can't protect you from his influence as long as the door is open. He's allowed to be there out of a judgement of God. Every sinful act is already judged and has a consequence attached to it. When we sin or surrender to the devil's influence on our carnal nature we expose ourselves to that judgement and are impacted by it until we repent before God and close that door. The only way to get rid of the judgement and close the door is to acknowledge the weakness as we take it to God. The Holy Spirit will pour Himself into this area of our life and fill it with His presence. ***This surrendered weakness gets filled with His presence and becomes your greatest strength because it is all God!*** This removes the devil's right to be there and he has to go.

Because this area of your life has been totally surrendered to God and you are very aware that you haven't got any natural ability (you have acknowledged that without God in that area of your life you would fail), it puts you in a position of total dependency on the inner working presence and power of the Holy Spirit. **Because it's all God, it becomes your greatest strength!**

God shows His great wisdom in this process. If our greatest power is in the surrendered weaknesses that are now filled with the Holy Spirit, in His wisdom, **He places us in a city that has strongholds that match our weaknesses.** When we rise above our areas of weakness in what I call our "personal spiritual supremacy," it brings a supernatural work of God into our lives that gives us the keys to minister to the violations of our city!

In a city or region the devil uses his temptations and influence to mess with our attitudes against the people and purposes of God. When we violate the principles of God it causes a breach in the hedge of protection and allows the enemy legal rights before God to be there. *He isn't stronger than God; he has found a violation or a doorway.*

Examples of Violations
and Corrections

The process of violations and corrections isn't directly stated in the Bible that I have seen, but it is there by example.

> *He who sins is of the devil, for the devil has sinned from the beginning. For this purpose the Son of God was manifested, <u>that He might destroy the works of the devil</u>.*

1 John 3:8

The reason Jesus came was to destroy what the devil had done. He came and did exactly what the Father wanted Him to do, and yet evil never left the earth.

The victory Jesus won in the wilderness never removed the devils, sin or sickness from the earth. It did, however, give him an anointing to fulfill the redemptive purpose on His life. He had a supernatural strength to go to the cross.

So what happened?

Jesus came to correct the violations created 1) in the heavenlies by Lucifer and 2) in the garden by man.

I have already mentioned the violations of the throne room and the garden of Eden. So how were these corrected?

In the Garden of Eden the devil tempted Adam and Eve with lust of the eyes, the lust of the flesh and the pride of life.

Jesus destroyed that work of the devil as He was led into the wilderness and was tested with the same things Adam was. Jesus did what Adam should have done at the point of testing; He stood on the word of God!

> *Then Jesus <u>returned in the power of the Spirit</u> to Galilee, and news of Him went out through all the surrounding region.*
>
> *Luke 4:14*

There was a new ministry anointing that had come into His life; a "personal spiritual supremacy!" I believe that every anointing that is released comes from passing the wilderness tests against the temptations of the devil. If we respond like Adam did and surrender to the temptations we may wander in that wilderness for years. What we surrender to shapes our lives, defines our influence and determines our destiny. If we do what Jesus did, we return in the power of the Spirit!

Before you go through the times of wilderness testing I would like to ask you... **Do you have a prayer shield?**

It is important to note at this time the power and protection of prayer. The rise of the prayer ministry in the church can bring blessing or division. It depends on the relationships and functions of the prayer teams you have.

One of the key teams is the prayer shield. Every leader needs to have people who are praying for them (especially when going through a process of finding and correcting a violation.) In our church we have a leadership chart that shows who the prayer shields are.

The prayer shield isn't there to get revelation or pray directional prayers. They have a specific function. I saw the pattern in the following passage:

> **And the Lord said, "Simon, Simon! Indeed, Satan has asked for you, that he may sift you as wheat. But I have prayed for you, _that your faith should not fail_; and when you have returned to Me, strengthen your brethren."**
>
> **Luke 22:31-32**

Jesus never said that He would stop the sifting from happening or that He would take care of it for Peter. He never even said, "I will be with you!" He said, "I'll pray that your faith won't fail!"

...This implies that your faith can fail!

This is the greatest prayer your prayer shield can pray for you: "Lord, I pray his faith won't fail!" When we are going through the wilderness times of testing the only thing that we need to stay focused on is that our faith in the Lord won't fail. Our words should be words of faith, proclaiming the prophecies we have received. Actions of faith show we believe even if we can't see, and a long lasting faith will stand against the testings and temptations of the devil. We need to keep in mind that Jesus is still in control and this season of testing shall pass! When it passes, a new anointing will get released.

..."**when you return**, strengthen the brethren!"

The wilderness and the rain barrel effects

There are at least two stages of leadership development as an individual rises to what I call personal spiritual supremacy.

The first is the **"wilderness experience,"** where the inner issues of life and our loyalty to the purposes of God are tested. At this stage you feel alone, one on one with life and the devil. Your relationships are tested, as well as your faith in the vision and your determination to succeed. You feel like you are in the desert—dry, alone and stretched by the pressures of life.

The second is what I call **"the rain barrel effect."** This is what you feel like when you return in a new power. I've heard it described in other terms like "rising to another level." When you rise to a new level or dimension of ministry the amount of experience and the anointing you carry that made you feel full and confident at the previous level now gets poured into a new dimension that is larger. I think of it as pouring a full 1-gallon pail into a larger container like a 45-gallon rain barrel. You haven't really lost anything at all, but it is in a larger space, so it makes you feel small and insecure. It has that hollow and vast sound like the emptiness of a rain barrel. At this point we have two choices. We can go back to the old dimension so we can feel full and confident, or we can allow others to pour into us at the new level until we fill up. You will return to that feeling of fullness and confidence if you will allow the process to be completed.

The keys to city transformation are found as we rise to a personal spiritual supremacy.

The new power that results from the wilderness experience will be the supernatural abilities needed to correct the violations before God and break the strongholds of your city.

The devil has convinced us to hide our weaknesses. This keeps us from getting that personal supremacy. This is why I believe it is critical that every Pastor has a Pastor! We need someone we trust that we can confide in, to help us rise to personal supremacy over our inner weaknesses. As long as the inner battle stays hidden and covered over, it remains a stronghold. We try to take our cities with our strengths but the keys are found in our *weaknesses that have been overcome by applying the word and have now become our strengths!*

Correcting the heavenly violation

We can see the process of violation and violation correction in the wilderness. Jesus did what Adam should have done; He stood on the word and resisted the devil until he left Him. But the greater violation of Lucifer (later to be known as the adversary or the devil) was in the throne room of God. He got an attitude of "pride." This created a violation in the heavenlies that also needed to be corrected.

Have you ever found yourself wondering why the cross? Why such an ugly death for such a great figure in history like Jesus? When I realized the reason Jesus came was to destroy the works of the devil, it started to make more sense. He could have spoke and changed the world. He could have called the angels of glory to fight on His behalf. Yet He didn't.

The angels stood silent and still.
The Father looked away.
The Son gave His life.

Why would He surrender to devils, to religious man and to life itself? Because this was an ultimate act of humility by the will and choice of an all-powerful and sovereign God!

It took an act of humility to correct the heavenly violation of pride!

For as the Father raises the dead and gives life to them, even so the Son gives life to whom He will. For the Father judges no one, but has committed all judgment to the Son...

John 5:21-22

All authority was given unto the Son! I have seen many people set free from fear as the revelation comes to them that the Father judges no one! There seems to be fear in the heart of man that God is some great judge of fire and brimstone in the sky. But the Father judges no one! We shouldn't have any fear of the Father (reverence, yes). As Christians we understand the grace and love of our Jesus, and He has been given the authority to judge all things in heaven and earth. This is eternal authority with total victory over every power of the enemy.

The great truth that we can draw from this scripture is that true spiritual authority is **not** gained by acts of aggression and strength that get those around to submit to our great abilities. *"True spiritual authority is gained by acts of humility!"*

> *And He sat down, called the twelve, and said to them, "If anyone desires to be first, he shall be last of all and <u>servant of all</u>."*
>
> *Mark 9:35*
>
> *And whoever of you desires to be first shall be slave of all.*
>
> *Mark 10:44*

A true apostolic leader will have a natural tendency and desire to serve. He will serve his sons and daughters to train and equip them to be able to **rise up higher and go farther** in spiritual and natural things than he or she ever did.

The greatness of a spiritual father is seen in how he treats his sons. If the sons are treated like servants by the leader, the leader may lead, but he will raise up servants, not sons and daughters! They may be faithful servants to follow instructions to the letter, but they will not be sons who are able to fulfill their own destiny before God.

This principle applies to team building dynamics that I will cover more in the chapter on the corporate anointing.

Other examples of violations and corrections can be seen in the Bible.

The instructions of the Lord to King Saul:

> *You shall go down before me to Gilgal; and surely I will come down to you to offer burnt offerings and make sacrifices of peace offerings. Seven days you shall wait, till I come to you and show you what you should do.*
>
> *1 Samuel 10:8*

The conditions of obedience:

> *If you fear the LORD and serve Him and obey His voice, and do not rebel against the commandment of the LORD, then both you and the king who reigns over you will continue following the LORD your God.*
>
> *However, if you do not obey the voice of the LORD, but rebel against the commandment of the LORD, then the hand of the LORD will be against you, as it was against your fathers.*
>
> *1 Samuel 12:14-15*

The test (conditions):

> *Then the Philistines gathered together to fight with Israel, thirty thousand chariots and six thousand horsemen, and people as the sand which is on the seashore in multitude. And they came up and encamped in Michmash, to the east of Beth Aven. When the men of Israel saw that they were in danger (for the people were distressed), then the people hid in caves, in thickets, in rocks, in holes, and in pits.*

And some of the Hebrews crossed over the Jordan to the land of Gad and Gilead. As for Saul, he was still in Gilgal, and all the people followed him trembling. Then he waited seven days, according to the time set by Samuel. But Samuel did not come to Gilgal; and the people were scattered from him.

1 Samuel 13:5-8

The choice:

So Saul said, "Bring a burnt offering and peace offerings here to me." And he offered the burnt offering. Now it happened, as soon as he had finished presenting the burnt offering, that Samuel came; and Saul went out to meet him, that he might greet him.

And Samuel said, "What have you done?"

And Saul said, "When I saw that the people were scattered from me, and that you did not come within the days appointed, and that the Philistines gathered together at Michmash...

1 Samuel 13:9-11

The cause:

"then I said, [NIV "I thought"] 'The Philistines will now come down on me at Gilgal, and I have not made supplication to the LORD.' Therefore I felt compelled, and offered a burnt offering.

1 Samuel 13:12

Saul relied on carnal thoughts and feelings instead

of just obeying God. (It is the same when we let natural circumstances influence our choices)

The judgement:

> **And Samuel said to Saul, "You have done foolishly. You have not kept the commandment of the LORD your God, which He commanded you. For now the LORD <u>would have established</u> your kingdom over Israel forever. But now your kingdom shall not continue. The LORD has sought for Himself a man after His own heart, and the LORD has commanded him to be commander over His people, because you have not kept what the LORD commanded you."**

> *1 Samuel 13:13-14*

This violation of Saul cost him his kingdom. At a point of pressure he relied on his thoughts and feelings (his carnal nature) instead of on the Word of the Lord. At a point of pressure one decision can determine your destiny. This is a *spirit or attitude of error* that I will cover in a later chapter. It was the same violation principle as Adam. He let the natural influence his obedience to the instructions of God, and the action brought a judgement.

Correcting this violation and fulfilling the mandate of God

The rest of this story is the interesting point I want to make. *V:14 says that God sought out for Himself a man after His own heart.*

If God just gave the kingdom to David without the

test, Saul would have had a legitimate complaint against God. It would be like this, "It was easier for David," or, "I had a lot more to deal with—he didn't have the same pressures, so no wonder he was able to make it." So the Lord arranged the situation to see if David would *pass the same test.*

> *Now it happened, when David and his men came to Ziklag, on the third day, that the Amalekites had invaded the South and Ziklag, attacked Ziklag and burned it with fire, and had taken captive the women and those who were there, from small to great; they did not kill anyone, but carried them away and went their way.*
>
> *So David and his men came to the city, and there it was, burned with fire; and their wives, their sons, and their daughters had been taken captive. Then David and the people who were with him lifted up their voices and wept, until they had no more power to weep. And David's two wives, Ahinoam the Jezreelitess, and Abigail the widow of Nabal the Carmelite, had been taken captive.*
>
> *Now David was greatly distressed, for the people spoke of stoning him, because the soul of all the people was grieved, every man for his sons and his daughters. But David strengthened himself in the LORD his God.*
>
> *Then David said to Abiathar the priest, Ahimelech's son, "Please bring the ephod here to me." And Abiathar brought the ephod*

to David. <u>So David inquired of the LORD, saying, "Shall I pursue this troop? Shall I overtake them?"</u>

And He answered him, "Pursue, for you shall surely overtake them and without fail recover all."

1 Samuel 30:1-8

David went through the same type of pressure Saul did, but he reacted and did what Saul should have done. He turned to God for instruction instead of relying on his own thoughts or feelings. This went against natural wisdom and ability and totally against the carnal nature. He was the leader. This was his city. This was his family. But in the point of great distress David rose above the natural and asked a totally unnatural faith question. *"<u>Shall I</u>* pursue this troop?" The implication here is that if God would have said no, David would have let them go!

David did what Saul should have done and it corrected the violation Saul had created. David's kingdom was established forever and the doorway of legal right for the devil was closed and the exposure to the judgement of God stopped! This created the Davidic anointing of our Christian heritage.

Transformation of a City!

In a region the same rules apply. I believe that the Lord had a reason for every city to come into existence in the first place. That redemptive purpose got shut down because of a violation to the principles of God. This created a breach in the hedge of protection and allowed the stronghold to be legally established.

*A key point to make is that it was an evil spirit **"of the Lord"** that came upon Saul.*

> *Then Samuel took the horn of oil and anointed him in the midst of his brothers; and the Spirit of the LORD came upon David from that day forward. So Samuel arose and went to Ramah. But <u>the Spirit of the LORD departed from Saul, and a distressing spirit from the LORD troubled him</u>. And Saul's servants said to him, "Surely, a distressing spirit <u>from God</u> is troubling you.*
>
> *1 Samuel 16:13-15*

The KJV puts it this way:

> **But the Spirit of the LORD departed from Saul, and _an evil spirit from the LORD_ troubled him. And Saul's servants said unto him, Behold now, an _evil spirit from God_ troubleth thee.**
>
> **1 Samuel 16:14-15**

This shows a violation against the instructions of God and the consequence of our wrong choices. It's something the body of Christ doesn't like to think about much, but it's important for us to know. When we violate the principles of God it's sin. God judges sin and through this judgement the devil gets legal rights to establish a presence.

It's the same for a church, for a city or even a nation!

God had a plan. Wrong decisions (that looked right in the natural) were made that violated that plan. A doorway was created. The judgement of God allowed legal right to demonic forces. The stronghold was established.

This stronghold is there because of the judgement of God and it's not going anywhere until we repent of the violation and get right with Him. When we do, the devil doesn't get a say—he loses his rights to be there, the doorways are closed and the kingdom advances in the will of God.

An intercessor that attended one of our "Power to Effect Change!" seminars used this illustration from _Romans 1:28..._

> **And even as they did not like to retain God in**

their knowledge, <u>God gave them over</u> to a debased mind, to do those things which are not fitting...

God gave them over to their own desires! So the regional climate would have been established, as this attitude of mind became the doorway for the devil. There would be a specific judgement that is relevant to the violation. He gave them over to it! We can shout at the devils all we want, but they don't have to leave our cities because of the violation and judgement.

Prayer is a key to success, but prayer has a greater purpose and impact when it is connected to jurisdictional or regional authority and the redemptive purposes of God! When we correct the violation ("Against you only have I sinned," David said) the whole region can be redeemed back into the purposes of God.

In Romans 8:3-4, Paul makes reference to violations and correction.

For what the law could not do in that it was weak through the flesh, [doorways] God did by sending His own Son in the likeness of sinful flesh, on account of sin: [violations] He condemned sin in the flesh, [judgement] that the righteous requirement of the law might be fulfilled [correction] in us who do not walk according to the flesh but according to the Spirit.

Again, here we can see an illustration of what I mean by violations and corrections. I believe that every sin is judged by God. As a Pastor I have found that I didn't have to protect myself from attacks from people. I found out that murmuring, gossip, rebellion and any other sin was already judged by God.

> *Then the LORD said to Moses: "How long will these people reject Me? And how long will they not believe Me, with all the signs which I have performed among them? <u>I will strike them</u> with the pestilence and disinherit them, and <u>I will make of you a nation greater and mightier than they</u>."*
>
> *Numbers 14:11-12*

God was willing to wipe them out for their disobedience and lack of faith!

> *Therefore the people came to Moses, and said, "We have sinned, for we have spoken against the LORD and against you; pray to the LORD that He take away the serpents from us." So Moses prayed <u>for the people</u>.*
>
> *Numbers 21:7*

We are to go before God **for the people not against them!** Sin is judged already!

In the ministry we can convince ourselves that we have to defend ourselves or fight off all the sinful people, words or actions. But in reality we are to go before God for them, not against them. The sin is judged already and without the grace of God there will be serious consequences. The judgement and consequence of sin doesn't come from the Pastor, but from God! We are to stand with our face towards

God and intercede for them.

The problem we have is that when we are standing with our face towards God, our backs are exposed to the people. Paul talks about the Christian armor and it was designed to protect you as you faced the enemy. The weakest area was on the back. If you turned around to run you were uncovered and exposed. Many of us as Pastors will turn around during a battle with people to try to defend ourselves, trying to use our gifts, personalities and confrontational skills to defeat the foe! We judge their actions and proclaim the consequences.

In reality, however, the judgement of God is already on their sin. He will already deal with it with more power and severity than we could anyway. We need to go before God for them and stand in the gap for His mercy, praying, "God these are your people!" instead of, "God help me, or protect me, or deal with them!"

If we turn inward to defend ourselves against people, we expose our backs, our weakest, most vulnerable area to the enemy. He waits for and tries to create this kind of situation. Then he can come at you from behind in your weaknesses rather than facing your strengths.

One of the greatest illustrations of our job as Pastors is seen in the following verse:

> **On the next day all the congregation of the children of Israel _murmured against Moses and Aaron_, saying, "You have killed the people of the LORD."**
>
> **Numbers 16:41**

I've heard Pastors that have said they are dying from sheep bite. They are referring to the words of the saints.

In the book of Job, chapter 1, we see the devil coming right into the throne room of God with the Saints. It's still the same today. The devil has no legal rights to be in a born-again church unless he is invited in and works through the saints!

In our words and attitudes towards each other, we give him a doorway to come right to the altar of God!

> **Now it happened, when the congregation had _gathered against Moses and Aaron_,** [sounds like a church split in the making!] **that they [Moses and Aaron] turned toward the tabernacle of meeting; and suddenly the cloud covered it, and the glory of the LORD appeared. Then Moses and Aaron came before the tabernacle of meeting.**
>
> **Numbers 16:42-43**

This is the right response for a leader, but it's hard to do. We naturally want to defend ourselves and prove we are right!

> **And the LORD spoke to Moses, saying,** [He got a word from God] **"Get away from among this congregation, that I may consume them in a moment."** [God's judgement]
>
> **Numbers 16:44-45**

Moses' response...And they fell on their faces.

Then Moses took action to stop the judgement of God against the people:

> **So Moses said to Aaron, "Take a censer and put fire in it from the altar, put incense on it, and <u>take it quickly to the congregation and make atonement for them</u>; (not against them!)for wrath has gone out from the LORD. The plague has begun."**

> **Then Aaron took it as Moses commanded, and ran into the midst of the assembly; and already the plague had begun among the people. So he put in the incense and made atonement for the people. <u>And he stood between the dead and the living; so the plague was stopped</u>.**

> **Numbers 16:46-48**

This is a perfect job description for the church!

We need to run out into our communities and stand between the dead and the living and stop the plagues of our society! Their sin is judged already—they need God's mercy and grace.

As Pastors we should position ourselves on the line between those who know the Lord and those who don't (the spiritually dead and the spiritually living) and stop the judgement of God from going any further.

However, there is a harsh reality that we need to be aware of. When we run out to stand between the dead and the living to stop the judgement of God, we have to be right with God ourselves or the judgement will affect us as well, taking us out and continuing on in the community!

This is what I call *apostolic work*—stopping the judgement of God against the community; going before God for the people and standing on the line between the dead and the living!

Two Dimensions of Apostolic Leadership

There are two dimensions of Apostolic leadership. One is *"authority"* and the other is *"influence."* The word authority has become a bad word in the body of Christ. But in reality it is a word we should cherish and hang on to. Authority has been used to defend ourselves or try to get our own way, but God never intended authority to be used for our own purposes. I see authority style leadership was used by Moses (and he was a very humble man). He was given the rod, which is a symbol of authority, and he used it to work a miracle by turning the river to blood. He used it to part the Red Sea and make a way for God's people where there seemed to be no way. He also used it to defend himself from the witchcraft of the Pharaoh's court.

> **Then the LORD spoke to Moses and Aaron, saying, "When Pharaoh speaks to you, saying, 'Show a miracle for yourselves,' then you shall say to Aaron, 'Take your rod and**

cast it before Pharaoh, and let it become a serpent.'"

So Moses and Aaron went in to Pharaoh, and they did so, just as the LORD commanded. And Aaron cast down his rod before Pharaoh and before his servants, and it became a serpent. But Pharaoh also called the wise men and the sorcerers; so the magicians of Egypt, they also did in like manner with their enchantments. For every man threw down his rod, and they became serpents. But Aaron's rod swallowed up their rods.

Exodus 7:8-12

The rod of authority isn't to rule over people. The rod of authority is over spiritual principalities and powers. We should live our lives in the protection of the authority of God!

We need to take up the rod of authority over the powers of the enemy to work the miracles of God, or to make a way where there seems to be no way. There is a place for leaders to rise up with the rod of authority and lead the people out of their bondage by the instructions of God. We all want someone to rise up and do these things on our behalf. The problem is that many times we try to use the same rod of authority to defend ourselves against those who would rise up against us.

Cast down the rod!

What the Lord showed me was that we are to use the rod the same way Moses did. We need to cast the rod of authority down between us and the serpents or the powers of man that come against us. **The key is cast it down.** That means we take our hands off.

Our natural tendency is to use the rod of authority like a weapon of defense instead of a shield of protection. If we don't release it or take our hands off of it, we limit God. He is only able to release as much of His power as we are able to have pass through us without killing us. So, instead of a flood of authority and power being released against the enemy, we see only a small portion. If He released the fullness of His power it would be like natural man trying to hang onto a tornado! The sheer power being released would tear us apart. So in His mercy, He uses only what we are able to handle, or only what we release through our ministries.

If we use the rod like Moses did and cast it down at our feet and take our hands off of it, it allows God to release the fullness of His power to do whatever needs to be done to consume the serpents and natural powers that are coming against us. This becomes our protection. We don't have to swing it like a stick, we only have to cast it down, take our hands off it and let the authority of God that we walk in be the protection in itself.

The key to leadership is to know that we can use **authority in the spirit realm,** but, for the most part, we can only use **influence in the natural realm**. You can't influence a devil and you can't force man. This book is about getting and **using the authority in the spirit realm** and walking through the doorways of **influence to man.**

Squirrel hunting with a bazooka

There is a process that happens as people start to rise in spiritual authority and increased anointing in their lives. They may go from being a Pastor of one church to Pastoring a city.

When the Lord answers that prayer and allows you the spiritual authority and influence you need to be successful, it comes with a greater responsibility and skill of how it is to be used.

I like to make this comparison. It's like being in city government one day and getting elected to provincial or national government the next. You are still the same person. You still have the same knowledge as you did the day before. But now the same words you spoke yesterday have greater impact. Why? Because now you are in a higher office!

It's the same in the spirit realm. When God gives you increase you have to be aware of what it is for. If you receive an anointing or an ability to Pastor a city, region or even a nation, and you use it to address local church troubles, it's **like going squirrel hunting with a bazooka.** The words you spoke yesterday that didn't seem to be too harsh now cut through the lives of people and can cause lasting damage to their spiritual life or their self-image. Using this greater anointing will definitely get rid of the problem but the devastation it causes around the problem will be worse and do more damage than the problem itself.

We have to be very conscious of this principle and not use a gifting of God that was intended for a city on an individual, or even a national anointing on one city!

Two Dimensions of Apostolic Leadership

The rod and the scepter

I see these principles and terms used in the Bible, and as I study them it appears they have much the same meaning.

The Strong's reference defines the same word for scepter as the rod. I still thought, however, that it would have a different meaning and purpose. I've heard it described as the rod symbolizes authority while the scepter describes power. We can have authority (by position) but not have any power (military might) to do anything with it, or we can have power without authority.

I think this is how it works.

We need both power and authority!

Police have authority because they have the law of the land on their side. The law of the land needs the co-operation of the majority of the people to have any effect. A fine is simply a penalty for a violation against the established will of the majority of the people.

So authority can be described as:

"Ruling by principles accepted and established by the majority."

Power, on the other hand, is when authority is forced or dictated over a people group without the accepted and established principles of the majority. This is rule without the free will of the followers, or forced acceptance.

So he answered and said to me: "This is the word of the LORD to Zerubbabel: 'Not by might nor by power, but by My Spirit,' Says the LORD of hosts."

Zechariah 4:6

I believe the Holy Spirit leads us into true authority by the accepted and established principles of the Word working in the hearts of the majority we lead.

With the co-operation of those who follow, it gives us the *scepter* of power, or to use a modern day word, **"Influence!"**

To put it in one statement I would say this:

Jurisdictional authority is...

"Ruling by principles of the Word accepted and established by the majority of those you lead." This co-operation of the corporate majority gives us the power of "Influence!"

The devil will do anything to stop the authority of God being released in this world!

He will do anything...and he has a new strategy to stop it from coming to pass.

I call his new strategy "Spiritual Terrorism!"

10

Spiritual Terrorism

I believe what we are seeing in the natural around the world is actually a reflection of the spiritual. The enemy has lost one of his greatest weapons to stop the body of Christ, "division." Pastors and leaders around the world are refusing to let division and strife separate us anymore. Without this weapon the devil's old strategies are in trouble. So I believe he has developed a new strategy. He is going for specific targets—high ones that are like the World Trade Center. These targets are ones that are seen by all, stand high above the rest, and it will cause fear in the hearts of the smaller or less established ministries if they are caused to fall.

Many will be attacked in areas of finances, hoping to stop the cash flow. One of our leaders made the observation that it wasn't the impact of the jet that caused the World Trade Centre to collapse, it just damaged and weakened the mainframe structure and the weight of the building fell in on itself. Many will get hit in their structures or organizational government in attempts to take out the mainframe so that the organization collapses in on itself. This is one of the reasons why unity in leadership is so important.

I asked my church members which one of them would be willing to be used by the enemy to fly the plane? Who would get on the plane of destruction and do nothing as it attacks the church? Who, on the other hand, would be like the heroes and say "No! I won't fly it, I won't get on it and if I find myself on it, I'll fly it into the ground!"

Many will be afraid to rise up to take leadership, knowing they will become targets, and many will just try to blend in and not be noticed. But one thing you can be sure of—there is an apostolic people alive today just as in Paul's day that will say "To live is Christ, to die is gain!" They will rise above the rest in spite of the risk. They will stand tall and continue to grow, and when the attacks come, **they will stand!**

There will be those who will rise up and rally the troops, organize the body of Christ and become an offensive initiative against the strategies of the devil. This is a new type of warfare for us, but it's not new for God. It forces us into the principles He designed in the beginning: unity, one cause greater than ourselves, one accord, prayer and a turning to Him for His presence to come.

The church is rising into its finest hour! The bride is being prepared for His return!

It will be a glorious church that is built out of people that know their God, who are strong and able to do great exploits!

This will take more than any single human or even one organization could do. It will take teamwork and co-operation in the body of Christ like never before.

There is one principle that is violated in the body of Christ more than any other. It's the principle of loyalty!

In the world I see people competing for position and building relationships based on opportunity and power. I understand it in the world, but I see the same principle at work in the body of Christ. When I see this relationship dynamic at work it looks like...

Monkeys swinging in the trees!

This principle is at work in human nature and it works in varying degrees in us all. It's the natural tendency to use someone until we get what we want or at least all we think they can do for us, then we look for the next relationship step up the ladder of success. Like "Monkeys swinging in the trees" we will swing on one branch of a tree (church or organization) until we get enough momentum or get introduced to and build a relationship with the next level and swing up to the next higher branch in another tree. This creates quite a problem when we are trying to raise up leaders to help us longterm. We pour our time and money into a potential leader and just when they are beginning to return some productive input into the organization, opportunity comes and they go for a higher branch in the forest.

If you are a leader of a major organization and grab hold of that one that is reaching up, you can pick up a new recruit that already has some training. This appears to be the right thing to do until they have taken all they can from you and there comes a higher branch than you and they go for it again. This process builds into the body of Christ a spirit of competition. It creates an environment that communicates that the only way to win is to be the highest tree in the forest (the largest church in town, the biggest organization, drawing the largest crowds, etc.).

It sounds funny, but it is a reality. We are all trying to be the biggest or the most dynamic so that others will join. We do it in our local church in our attitudes towards the other churches in our city. We say we really don't want the people from another church, but in truth, we turn very few of them away. We get the attitude that the church down the street wasn't feeding them or that we have special favor from God. We still get recognized as the model of success because of the large numbers of people in attendance, even if building our large church meant that twenty-five smaller churches ceased to exist.

The combined pressure to succeed or to survive the financial pressures of ministry and the gauge of success based on numbers forces us to be guarded. It stops a smaller or less experienced leader from connecting his or her church or organization by relationship to another one that is larger or more experienced because they really can lose leaders and people, rather than gain strength and support.

I believe the responsibility is on the greater to stop the process. If a larger tree in the forest wants to get involved, they should do all they can to help the existing apostolic leader or Pastor to be better equipped to train other leaders under them.

I see whole organizations that have had an apostolic father figure help them succeed for years until they grow to a place where they feel they don't need him anymore or where they feel that he doesn't have the knowledge to help. Then they shut him out of the process and grab hold of another organization or leader that they feel has the present day truth to succeed.

You can see this principle at work in conferences. I was working at a leadership conference a few years ago and was asked if I would drive one of the guest ministries to one of the sessions. On the way this guest thought I was just a driver or servant, so he treated me with very short and direct instructions of what I had to do for him. When we arrived at the meeting and he found out that I was the host of the service and one of the speakers at the conference he treated me in a totally different way.

In our organization it is mandatory that every Pastor has a Pastor. My Pastor is Pastor Mel Mullen of the Word of Life Church in Red Deer, Alberta. When I travel with my Pastor, I watch how other leaders treat me. They have a reason to treat my Pastor well because he might invite them to speak at his national conference or other ministry opportunities around the world. If they see me as his servant some of them will pay very little attention to me. A true father of the faith will treat another man's servant, and especially a spiritual son, with just as much, if not more honor than a peer. I am pleased to say I have met some great, true, fathers and mothers of the faith!

Another thing you can watch at a conference is that everyone starts out equal. We are all equal until there is a knowledge of who you are, what influence you have or haven't got, what success you have achieved and whether or not you have something that will be to their advantage or build their ministry by establishing a relationship with you. Within hours of arrival the separation process goes through the crowd like oil and water and soon there are those that won't even stand and talk with a seemingly lesser minister. Again, I see the social climbing like a political game being played by monkeys swinging in the trees.

When we see other people doing it we call it pride, but when it's us, we call it a door of opportunity the Lord has opened.

The reason I say this is that the spiritual keys for our town were put into the hands of people we could have seen as insignificant and unimportant with nothing to contribute to our success.

The Lord tested our hearts to honor those who serve who don't appear to be the movers or shakers of society. If we had seen them as unimportant or lesser in any way, this book wouldn't have been written, because *God packed the knowledge into a box that could only be opened by people with the right heart towards those that serve.*

I believe that we need to watch for the servants like David who are just being faithful with the Father's sheep. They are the ones that God will trust with greatness, not the ones that appear to be a head and shoulders above the rest.

So, instead of watching and swinging for the higher branch, stick with your family and nurture your own tree so that one day it may be the largest tree in the forest. The strength and nourishment we are looking for doesn't come from the higher branches—it comes from the roots! **Stay connected to your roots!**

In the next chapters I want to address a principle I see in the Bible that I call **"the corporate anointing**!"

11

Key #3—The Corporate Anointing

There are many types of local church and organizational government structures, and many illustrations to show how they work in the kingdom of God. Some are Pastor-run, some board-run, some are elderships and some are congregational. All have their strengths and all have a logical and practical reason for why they are structured that way.

These government structures have a democratic, systematic approach to problem solving, financial control and direction of the church. However, I believe we have become part of the *"kingdom"* of God, not a democracy! A kingdom has a King! It has servants! It has those that rule over tens, those over hundreds and those over thousands! I know the King is Jesus, but I believe that there is also a kingdom governmental order being established on the earth today. This involves a relational covering by a more seasoned minister than yourself (i.e. every Pastor having a Pastor). This accountability is built into the structure at the same time as having self-governing principles or autonomy. The local church functions in a team dynamic that I will expand on later.

There is governmental order in the spirit realm starting with the Trinity to the Seraphim and Cherubim, to Michael, Gabriel and originally Lucifer, then the angels and finally, man.

There are also governmental structures in the devil's kingdom. These are counterfeit or pattern copies of Gods kingdom.

The three main powers or spirits I believe we are dealing with in the spirit realm are:

1. The spirit of Leviathan (spirit of error) influencing the minds of men.

2. The spirit of strife that robs the harvest.

3. The spirit of rebellion that works like witchcraft.

These spiritual forces are what we battle, not man!

For we do not wrestle against flesh and blood, but against principalities, against powers, against the rulers of the darkness of this age, against spiritual hosts of wickedness in the heavenly places.

Ephesians 6:12

The spiritual realm has ruling powers or governments the same as the natural world has. The Bible is full of the terminology of governmental authority. As mentioned early, we too often avoid using the word authority because it has been abused so much. Regardless, abuse of authority doesn't change the fact that authority and governmental accountability is a solid principle of the Word.

> **Remember those <u>who rule over you</u>, who have spoken the word of God to you, whose faith follow, considering the outcome of their conduct.**
>
> *Hebrews 13:7*

> **Obey those <u>who rule over you</u>, and be submissive, for they watch out for your souls, as those who must give account. Let them do so with joy and not with grief, for that would be unprofitable for you.**
>
> *Hebrews 13:17*

> **Greet all those <u>who rule over you</u>, and all the saints. Those from Italy greet you.**
>
> *Hebrews 13:24*

Even the thought that we are called to join the **army** of the Lord and that He is the Captain of the hosts, implies a structure and form of governmental order.

I describe 'covering' this way: "Those whom I have asked to watch over me, teach me what I need to learn and hold me accountable so I don't hurt myself or the people God sends me."

This is also true for our local church. We have a government structure that involves relational accountability without removing the self-governing principles of the teams. Each team in our church has the same accountability principles in place.

We have developed a formula we use in our prayer teams:

"Prophetic revelation, confirmed by natural knowledge and released by permission."

Here's how it works (I will use our family prayer team as an example):

We use prayer request forms that are given to our prayer Pastor and then to the prayer teams. As they start to pray for that family, revelations or impressions start to come. We tend to think that as one person gets a revelation and another agrees, it must be right because we have had a witness or an agreement. The fact is that *we can have many who think it's right and still not be right*. If they continue to pray in this direction they can actually be praying a new problem onto someone instead of removing one.

So we use this formula. When a witness comes that we have discerned the root of the problem we stop there and get it confirmed with natural knowledge before we go on. That means that the discernment comes back to me on the prayer reports I get from the prayer Pastor and we do what we can to confirm it with the family or individual.

If the discernment gets confirmed by the family and proves accurate we still don't have permission to go after it. The family may have too many other issues they are dealing with already so they can't deal with that one right now. If that happens, we put it on the shelf until they are ready. On the other hand, if they say yes, then we have *the revelation*, which has been *confirmed by natural knowledge*, that it is accurate for that family and that season of time, and we now have *their permission* to tear it down. That gives us prayer with governmental power with all stakeholders in agreement. Church authority never overrides family authority, so we need parental agreement and permission.

We have had prayer working in the local church for years with hit and miss success. It's like a shotgun blast into the dark, and once in a while we even hit something. When we have accurate discernment confirmed with natural knowledge and released by permission of those involved along with the leadership of the church, it **becomes a targeted missile into the enemy's camp!**

On a larger scale, we need the church intercessors to get accurate discernment for the city that can be confirmed with natural historical knowledge. Eighty percent of intercession is research. This information then goes to the local church government to determine the wisdom, timing and strategies needed. It then gets released by permission as an apostolic proclamation. This is targeted city prayer with governmental power!

I see the governmental terminology and military form in Daniel 10 as we see a messenger sent from heaven.

> *Suddenly, a hand touched me, which made me tremble on my knees and on the palms of my hands. And he said to me, "O Daniel, man greatly beloved, understand the words that I speak to you, and stand upright, for I have now been sent to you." While he was speaking this word to me, I stood trembling. Then he said to me, "Do not fear, Daniel, for from the first day that you set your heart to*

understand, and to humble yourself before your God, your words were heard; and I have come because of your words. "<u>But the prince of the kingdom of Persia withstood me twenty-one days; and behold, Michael, one of the chief princes, came to help me</u>, for I had been left alone there with the kings of Persia. "Now I have come to make you understand what will happen to your people in the latter days, for the vision refers to many days yet to come."

Daniel 10:10-14

It's very important we learn how to fight and win against the devils. Where are we going to win? How will we ever learn? It's in the local church!

And He Himself gave some to be apostles, some prophets, some evangelists, and some pastors and teachers, for the equipping of the saints for the work of ministry, for the edifying of the body of Christ...

Ephesians 4:11-12

I call the local church "Boot Camp!" In military boot camp or in any kind of rescue training, there is a great effort made to have mock wars or mock disasters. These mock events are intentionally created as realistic as possible without endangering the lives of the people. This is done so that when we get out into the real disaster or war, we will respond according to our training. The noise, confusion or any other element of the circumstance won't be foreign to us and we will respond by training instead of stopping to have a meeting to decide what needs to be done. If you don't know what to do before the battle begins, you have very little chance of surviving even a weak enemy.

God does the same in the local church. When we pray and ask God for our city He has to train us for the work of the ministry.

He starts a boot camp! A mock war with all the elements of the real thing but a place where nobody dies. We might sound like we are dying, but we aren't! If we were sent out into the real battle we would get hurt or hurt others. God sends us first to be trained in a mock war environment that reflects the spiritual dynamic of our city. When we learn how to overcome in the mock war He releases us into the real one. In this camp we learn how to deal with the devils and identify the doorways of carnality that let them in. As we learn how to effectively deal with them in the local church (where it is a relatively safe place to be), then God can send us out to our community to deal with the real battles.

In Daniel, when the spiritual war was on Michael came to help the messenger angel win the battle. It's the same in the local church. God sends those who can come alongside the one with the message from God or the vision. They form the local church government by relationship and teamwork.

These helpers are keys to our success because the only way to defeat a governing authority in the spirit realm is with a stronger government!

"It takes a government to replace a government!"

Those that come alongside us are the government of God for our church, and as we join together with other churches it establishes the government for our city; and as organizations join it becomes the spiritual government of our nation!

The corporate church has the greatest responsibility before God for the future and well being of our cities and our nation.

> **Now it shall come to pass in the latter days That <u>the mountain of the LORD'S house Shall be established on the top of the mountains</u>, And shall be exalted above the hills; And peoples shall flow to it. Many nations shall come and say, "Come, and let us go up to the mountain of the LORD, To the house of the God of Jacob...**

> **Micah 4:1-2**

This is symbolic writing referring to God's government! In the last days, ("now") the spiritual government of the Lord's house will be established above the other powers.

We see demonic forces being released on the face of the earth today! *We can be afraid or we can be inspired!* The church of the Lord Jesus Christ is coming alive! It's entering its finest hour! God is bringing order and government to the corporate church that will **release authority** to the anointings already here. We will see prayers go *from prophetic revelations to apostolic proclamations!* Job 22 says, "Declare a thing and it will be established for you!" I call this going from **"Prophetic revelations to an Apostolic reality"** by bringing the spiritual discernment into a tangible functioning reality in the natural world.

We have tried to inspire faith over the years and I believe we should continue, but in reality inspiring faith alone doesn't take cities or change nations. *It takes a government to replace a government.*

The early church disciples were hand-picked by Jesus himself. They were *the government of God* for the new church age. When Jesus won the battle we read about in Luke chapter 4 and got what I call "personal spiritual supremacy" (He returned in the power), He used the new ability in His life to establish the twelve disciples. The number twelve is a symbol of government!

They were the New Testament government, but they didn't know what they had.

> **And when they had come to the multitude, a man came to Him, kneeling down to Him and saying, "Lord, have mercy on my son, for he is an epileptic and suffers severely; for he often falls into the fire and often into the water. So I brought him to Your disciples, but they could not cure him."**
>
> **Then Jesus answered and said, "O faithless and perverse generation, how long shall I be with you? How long shall I bear with you? Bring him here to Me."**
>
> **And Jesus rebuked the demon, and it came out of him; and the child was cured from that very hour. Then the disciples came to Jesus privately and said, "Why could we not cast it out?"**

So Jesus said to them, "Because of your unbelief; for assuredly, I say to you, if you have faith as a mustard seed, <u>you will say to this mountain,</u> 'Move from here to there,' and it will move; and nothing will be impossible for you. However, this kind does not go out except by prayer and fasting."

Matthew 17:14-21

We tend to think that Jesus was referring to a mountain in the distant horizon when He said "move from here to there." In fact, though, He was referring to the spiritual or demonic force of epilepsy.

They had the governmental authority to command that demon to go, they just didn't know what they had. They were the government or authority of God. This is also what Ananias and Saphirra came in contact with. They lied to the Spirit in the presence of the governmental authority of God and judgement was served instantly. We don't have the power over demons today like we should and we don't have the strong presence of the Spirit of God *because we don't have government.* What we call government today is really just administration. We need that, too, but what I'm talking about goes beyond administration to *a spiritual authority with...*

"The Power to Effect Change!"

The fasting and prayer referred to in verse 21 that is needed is really just a part of the process toward spiritual authority! When we fast it brings our being back into order. We re-train our body and our mind to listen and obey our spirit that is filled with God's Spirit.

This brings a personal spiritual supremacy and order in us that releases the authority and power needed to move spiritual mountains. In this way fasting is really a retraining and strengthening of our being which increases the awareness and release of the Spirit of God! The glory of God is still hidden behind the veil, which is the flesh. When we fast it brings order and realigns our being. We were created to walk in the spirit, with our spirit feeding and leading our soul. Our flesh is to be the lowest nature. This applies to the individual as well as to cities or nations. In our fallen state we are being led by the flesh, which feeds our soul and keeps the spirit starving and dead. When we fast and pray it brings our being into proper order and turns us right side up again so that we are walking with God in spirit and truth. As the soul is under the control of the spirit, which is in communion with God's Spirit, it keeps the lowest nature, the flesh, in order and reveals more of the glory of God that is in us.

The disciples of Jesus' day were just like us today. They were trying to be people of faith! We are always trying to stir up faith, but in reality the Bible says that faith as a grain of mustard seed would have defeated this mountain (the demonic force of epilepsy). The issue is, are you walking in authority? Faith can and needs to be built but authority needs to be obtained. Your authority is established as you connect to Him and His plans. Your faith is built when He connects with you.

Look at what Jesus said:

And again He entered Capernaum after some days, and _it was heard that He was in_

__the house__. Immediately many gathered together, so that there was no longer room to receive them, not even near the door. And He preached the word to them. Then they came to Him, bringing a paralytic who was carried by four men. And when they could not come near Him because of the crowd, they uncovered the roof where He was. So when they had broken through, they let down the bed on which the paralytic was lying. When Jesus __saw their faith__, He said to the paralytic, "Son, your sins are forgiven you."

Mark 2:1-5

Faith is something we can see! James wrote, "faith without works is dead!" We all try to stir up our faith. We even have an attitude that says, "if I can just have enough faith and do the right things, the Lord will show up!"

Most of our North American churches have this dynamic in our services. The music is timed and planned to touch the heart of God and men, and the atmosphere of reverence is sought after like a god itself. The message is challenging, yet careful not to be offensive, we sing about freedom and liberty but have more programs to control the service than the city government.

We need structure and order, but I see in the early church, like the church at Corinth, a group of people that didn't have any of these things, but they had something that most of our churches don't have— miracles, signs and wonders and explosive growth! Why? We think that they had greater faith or some other thing that made them great, but in Mark 2:1 we see the real reason the early disciples had so many people coming to church. **"It was heard that Jesus was in the house!"** The presence of Jesus caused people to do exceptional acts of faith. They didn't do acts of faith in hopes that Jesus would come; **Jesus was there and it inspired great acts of faith!"**

The only real issue of church growth and success is this one, *"Is Jesus in the house?"*

If He is there in a real and tangible way, the music can be less than great, the message simple salvation, but the inspiration of our faith, miraculous!

We need to encourage and build faith, but the fastest and most impacting way to build a church is to have people experience Jesus in a real and tangible way!

In **Acts 1:3** we see that Jesus went out of His way to show Himself to His disciples:

> *...to whom He also presented Himself alive after His suffering by many <u>infallible proofs</u>, being seen by them during forty days and speaking of the things pertaining to the kingdom of God.*

There were many infallible or unmistakable truths that He was there. I believe Jesus will do the same for us. We shouldn't have to have board meetings to figure out if what happened last Sunday was God or not!

There is a time coming when God's presence will be so strong in the house that *the devil won't be able to copy it , the people won't be able to deny it and the church won't be able to contain it!*

There's a time coming when the fire of God will come to the house and purge sin, win the youth, set the captives free, heal the sick and the Pastors will proclaim, as Elijah did:

> **And it came to pass, at the time of the offering of the evening sacrifice, that Elijah the prophet came near and said, "LORD God of Abraham, Isaac, and Israel, let it be known this day <u>that You are God in Israel and I am Your servant, and that I have done all these things at Your word</u>."**
>
> *1 Kings 18:36*

In **Matthew 16:20** the Lord said that He would confirm His Word with signs following!

> **And they went out and preached everywhere, the Lord working with them and confirming the word through the accompanying signs. Amen.**

I know the presence of God comes from reverence and commitment and all the other things we teach—I'm not saying these things aren't important! But I am saying that the presence can be there without the power being released.

We have seen people come to a meeting for the first time and have a life-changing experience with the Lord. At the same time we pray for the sick and see very little of the "unmistakable proof" that our prayers are answered. So we all tend to pray safe prayers like "Thy will be done Lord!" This is so that if the healing doesn't come they can't blame the Pastor!

I don't want to minister in a realm of hopes and maybes or the gray areas of "If it is Thy will Lord." I want an unmistakable presence of God in the house that inspires acts of faith! I want everyone to see Him confirm His Words we speak with signs following! To me, **that's church!**

I was a preacher of faith for many years. I always thought if we could just believe enough, then Jesus would come to answer our faith. There is an element of truth to that thought that I don't want to lose. But I found that there is even a greater element needed than great faith, it's His presence. When we know beyond any doubt that He is there, faith will be easy!

When we have His presence it inspires our faith. He leads us to the place of Kadesh (or holiness) just like he did with the people in the wilderness. At the place of holiness He will show us the Promised Land. So the process is this: His presence leads us to holiness and inspires our faith. At the place of holiness He shows us the promises but we have to exercise our faith to posses them.

This book is all about the keys to His presence in our cities. In the next section I want to expand on the principles of the corporate anointing.

The Government
of God

For unto us a Child is born, Unto us a Son is given; <u>And the government will be upon His shoulder</u>. And His name will be called Wonderful, Counselor, Mighty God, Everlasting Father, Prince of Peace. <u>Of the increase of His government and peace There will be no end</u>, Upon the throne of David and over His kingdom, To order it and establish it with judgment and justice From that time forward, even forever. The zeal of the LORD of hosts will perform this.

Isaiah 9:6-7

We all know that Jesus is the head of the church. That means the body starts with the shoulders! **"And the government shall be upon His shoulders!"**

There is a government structure in the spirit realm. There is terminology of family and tribe or army, along with the instructions to honor those who rule over us in the Lord and many other areas and examples of scripture to enforce the concept of governmental order.

We see it in the natural realms of the home, the school systems, the business community and politics, but in the church we struggle with it. We don't want to think that someone else will rule over us because this makes us think of control or dictatorship. But Jesus showed us it was neither of these. It is having a heart of a servant but the spiritual authority of a warrior.

The scripture I quoted already from Micah 4 about the mountain of the Lord's house being established upon the other mountains, goes on to say...

> **But in the last days it shall come to pass, that the mountain of the house of the LORD shall be established in the top of the mountains, and it shall be exalted above the hills; and _people shall flow unto it_. And many nations shall come, and say, Come, and let us go up to the mountain of the LORD, and _to the house of the God of Jacob_...**
>
> _Micah 4:1-2_

People will flow to it! Because of the increased presence of the Lord. It's the greatest evangelism strategy we can have!

Notice that it says the house of the God of Jacob rather than the house of Abraham the father of faith. There are probably many reasons for this but here's one possibility.

Abraham received the covenant promises. These promises were tested by God. In Genesis 12, God made a covenant promise to Abraham. Then Abraham was tested. He was asked to put that promise on the altar and sacrifice it to God in chapter 22. This tested Abraham's faith in God, his determination and everything about his natural man. He passed the test and the covenant promise became a reality in his life.

We have the same process today. We can read the promises and blessings of God or we get a prophecy that shows we are called to a ministry or some other great calling of God. This promise remains only words until it is tested. When it gets tested and we respond with faith and dedication to the Lord, it becomes ours and is an established principle or anointing in our life.

Any anointing you see working in a person's life is there by passing through the fire of testing by God. When you are tested and stand true to the Lord, you will return in the power of the Spirit!

Abraham got the promise; Isaac was the seed of that promise that was planted by faith at the altar. Isaac's son, Jacob, rose up the twelve sons, or, in other words, he birthed the government of the Old Testament!

I believe that the Lord is calling us to government! Not to natural government and politics, but to order in the house of the Lord and in the Body of Christ in general. If this is true then we need some leaders in our government. These generals (or whatever natural title would describe them) are what I call the Apostles of God!

These Apostles aren't of the order of the original

twelve, but are more in the apostolic order of those who came after them.

They will rally the troops, sound the battle cry, identify the enemy, gather the information and develop the strategy to break down the strongholds of the enemy. By this they will lead our cities into their redemptive purpose.

In Acts 2 we see the great outpouring of the Holy Spirit. I don't believe that it stopped! He is still flowing out from heaven the same today! He is over all the earth with equal intensity. He is the same Holy Spirit who is winning souls and working miracles in any geographical location we can name! The work He does to prepare us for His coming is seen in Acts 1. The issues were unity, prayer, fellowship and one accord. He is stirring the same issues today in the Body of Christ. As we learn to work together as one, with one heart and one sound, we will see heaven bow down and touch earth. This will take a team effort that I have called the corporate anointing.

There is a great place and need for the unity movement in our cities. But it's not to get us up into the presence of the Lord—it's to bring His presence down. Another way of saying it would be to bring His spiritual presence into a tangible natural presence.

Heaven bows down!

There is some wording in scripture that inspired the next thought about the corporate anointing.

Bow down Your heavens, O LORD, and come down; Touch the mountains, and they shall smoke.

Psalms 144:5

He bowed the heavens also, and came down
With darkness under His feet.

Psalms 18:9

He bowed the heavens also, and came down
with darkness under His feet.

2 Sam 22:10

There are many theologies about these scriptures and the possible interpretations. I'm not a theologian, but here is what it inspired in me.

I believe that the heavens will bow down by the corporate anointing and the government of God.

So then, after the Lord had spoken to them, He was received up into heaven, and sat down at the right hand of God.

Mark 16:19

For you died, and your life is hidden with Christ in God.

Colossians 3:3

So we are hidden in Christ, the Anointed One, and in His anointing (safest place to stay—in the anointing). It puts us at the right hand of God! So I would say this: **We can't get any higher or any closer to God the Father than we are in Christ Jesus!** When we are born-again Christians we are in Christ at the right hand of God.

Most of our spiritual warfare approach to the Daniel chapter 10 principalities and powers is done from street level up toward this great spiritual force in the sky, but in fact, the devil is under our feet in Jesus! **He's down, not up!** We should do all spiritual warfare from the top down, not the bottom up!

Our job as Christians isn't to work our way through the powers of darkness into the presence of God! We're already there! **Our job is to bring that presence to the natural or the street level of experience!** This is what I see in the Scriptures about heaven bowing down!

The Apostle Paul talks about the body ministry in *1 Corinthians 12:12-28...*

> *For as the body is one and has many members, but all the members of that one body, being many, are one body, so also is Christ. For by one Spirit we were all baptized into one body——whether Jews or Greeks, whether slaves or free——and have all been made to drink into one Spirit. For in fact the body is not one member but many.*
>
> *If the foot should say, "Because I am not a hand, I am not of the body," is it therefore not of the body? And if the ear should say, "Because I am not an eye, I am not of the body," is it therefore not of the body? If the whole body were an eye, where would be the hearing? If the whole were hearing, where would be the smelling?*
>
> *But now God has set the members, each one of them, in the body just as He pleased. And if they were all one member, where would the body be? But now indeed there are many members, yet one body.*

And the eye cannot say to the hand, "I have no need of you"; nor again the head to the feet, "I have no need of you." No, much rather, those members of the body which seem to be weaker are necessary. And those members of the body which we think to be less honorable, on these we bestow greater honor; and our unpresentable parts have greater modesty, but our presentable parts have no need. But God composed the body, having given greater honor to that part which lacks it, <u>that there should be no schism in the body, but that the members should have the same care for one another</u>.

And if one member suffers, all the members suffer with it; or if one member is honored, all the members rejoice with it.

<u>*Now you are the body of Christ, and members individually*</u>*. And God has appointed these in the church: <u>first apostles</u>, second prophets, third teachers, after that miracles, then gifts of healings, helps, administrations, varieties of tongues.*

I see in this important passage of scripture **the foundation for releasing the corporate anointing!** We are all one body and each one has a part to play in the purposes of God!

The greatest reason to be a part of the church is to see every expression of God in action. Those that prophesy, those that work miracles, those that preach, do deliverance or whatever else is needed to follow the redemptive purpose are found in the house! When we work together we see more of the fullness of God released. It also is a protection for us. In the corporate church there are those who are responsible before God to protect the sheep from the wolves and keep sound doctrines even in a "divine disorder" environment! Those carrying the responsibility are called the pastors. Those who take and carry the responsibility are given the authority— they are not necessarily the most gifted ones.

People working together, each one flowing in his or her strength, yet working in total harmony with, and accountable to the others, releases a greater presence and power of God and that's what I call the corporate anointing.

This works in a city as well! The word 'glory' has many meanings, but one of them that applies in this context is "His weighty presence!"

We all want the glory of God to fall on our personal lives, our churches and our cities or nations. The weighty presence of God with us! It can and it will come if we will work together!

What I see in the spirit realm is like a canopy that we are standing on in the heavenlies. The weight of my presence, gifting and the anointing He has given causes the canopy to sag a little. When someone else comes and stands with me in harmony and agreement it adds his or her weight to mine and causes the canopy to sag a little more. As more people come to stand with us, it adds more weight to the canopy and it lowers each time weight is added!

In a city whole churches can unite in unity and harmony to add their weighty presence to the canopy until the united weighty presence of God gets so heavy it causes **the canopy of heaven to bow down to earth** and the weighty presence of the God of heaven is like thick air and can be felt on the earth!

This isn't suggesting that God isn't here right now or that He is sitting out past Pluto somewhere. What I am talking about is experiencing a manifest presence of God, as the reality of the spirit realm crosses over or bows down into the natural.

I believe the Lord has developed a system that He works sovereignly in to force us into unity if we want His presence!

If we remain independent, isolated or offended, our weight doesn't get added to our city and the canopy of God either won't bow low enough in the first place or will lift when division comes.

Acts 1 shows the issues of unity, one accord, fellowship and prayer. These are all important issues of relationship to see the glory of God fall or the canopy of heaven bow down!

When the canopy of light bows down to earth, it pushes back the powers of darkness that rule and reign and they are displaced by the glory!

Think about it! **Darkness can't be projected, it is simply the absence of light!**

Don't chase darkness...
"Turn on the Lights!"

When we "Turn on the lights" of the redemptive purposes of God (the reason the city exists in the first place), the darkness is overcome. Devils are creatures of darkness. When the lights come on they will scurry into the shadows, therefore they are displaced as the ruling power over a city.

So, true apostolic government is to bring order and unity by helping each person and ministry find the reason they exist or their redemptive purpose. The next step is to find out how it works in harmony with the rest of the body, adding their weighty presence to the canopy of God.

This is why the devil works so hard at division and strife. He knows he can't stop the anointing of God under a combined government of authority and strategy. All he can do is to try to keep us from uniting to build that government by keeping us independent, offended, prideful or anything else that will keep us apart!

We bought a horse one time and when we put her with the other horses the rest of the herd chased her around and seemed to be cruel to her for about three days. The man that looked after the horses said that they were just establishing the "pecking order." I asked him what he meant. He said, "They will challenge her until she finds what place in the herd she belongs, then they will run in unity as a group." Three days later I saw her right in the middle like she had always been there. The larger horses or the stallions watched over her as she went about just being herself.

I saw in this that God has placed even in nature an understanding of order. Nature works it out. Man just gets offended and walks in pride thinking, "No one is over me." But in reality, having someone over us is Bible.

Therefore I did not even think myself worthy to come to You. But say the word, and my servant will be healed. For I also am <u>a man placed under authority,</u> having soldiers under me. And I say to one, 'Go,' and he goes; and to another, 'Come,' and he comes; and to my servant, 'Do this,' and he does it."

When Jesus heard these things, He marveled at him, and turned around and said to the crowd that followed Him, "I say to you, <u>I have not found such great faith, not even in Israel!</u>"

Luke 7:7-9

The man understood authority because he was under authority. Jesus related this to faith!

I like to use this illustration about authority.

When a small police officer stops a big mean person, how come they don't just take that little policeman by the neck and throw him in the ditch? We all know that the reason is that they are representing and have the authority of the land behind them. To challenge the officer would be to challenge the authority behind them.

It's the same in the spiritual realm. When you have relational authority watching over you, it adds that person's strength and power to yours. If the devil wants to challenge you he has to take them on at the same time, too. The corporate anointing under the government of God brings a protection and a greater release of authority and power in the heavenlies. We use the authority that God has given us at the same time as we tap into the spiritual authority of those that rule over us in the Lord.

Watch for the mantle to fall

One of the greatest reasons to function in the corporate anointing is so we can see what the Holy Spirit is doing and the gifts He is stirring in a very clear way.

> **And so it was, when they had crossed over, that Elijah said to Elisha, "Ask! What may I do for you, before I am taken away from you?"**
>
> **Elisha said, "Please let a <u>double portion of your spirit be upon me</u>."**
>
> **2 Kings 2:9**

This is impartation! We receive from those that carry an ability or an anointing from God.

In **1 Samuel 10:10-11** we see the Spirit of the Lord come on Saul to prophecy as he was with the prophets:

> **When they came there to the hill, there was a group of prophets to meet him; <u>then the Spirit of God came upon him, and he prophesied among them</u>. And it happened, when all who knew him formerly saw that he indeed prophesied among the prophets, that the people said to one another, "What is this that has come upon the son of Kish? Is Saul also among the prophets?"**

We can receive from a Prophet or any other gifting of God by working with the ministries that have them. It's called "impartation."

Elisha asked Elijah for a double portion of what he saw in his mentor.

So he said, "You have asked a hard thing. Nevertheless, if you see me when I am taken from you, it shall be so for you; but if not, it shall not be so."

Then it happened, as they continued on and talked, that <u>suddenly a chariot of fire appeared with horses of fire</u>, and separated the two of them; and Elijah went up by a whirlwind into heaven.

And Elisha <u>saw it</u>, and he cried out, "My father, my father, the chariot of Israel and its horsemen!" So he saw him no more. And he took hold of his own clothes and tore them into two pieces. He also took up the mantle of Elijah that had fallen from him, and went back and stood by the bank of the Jordan.

Then he took the mantle of Elijah that had fallen from him, and struck the water, and said, "Where is the LORD God of Elijah?" And when he also had struck the water, it was divided this way and that; and Elisha crossed over.

2 Kings 2:10-14

He walked with the man of God, he saw the fire of God, he saw the mantle fall and he picked it up and used it to perform the same miracles that Elijah had done.

This is a great example of impartation and covering. When we work with someone who is over us in the Lord with an attitude to serve, a heart to receive and an eye to see the fire, we are ready for impartation.

In every service you can see the fire or the flow of the Spirit of God if you watch for it. When you see the fire like Elisha did, follow the fire and watch for the mantle to fall. When the mantle falls pick it up! Just seeing it doesn't do anything if you just let it lay there. Pick it up and use it to do the same things you saw them do with it.

I hear many say, "Where is the God of Elijah?"

I say, "Where are the Elijah's and Elisha's of God?!" They are those who can see the fire and carry the mantle to perform the miracles.

Apostolic fathers of today are in the process of establishing governmental authority in the body of Christ worldwide.

I see two dimensions of leadership being established at the same time. There are those who have poured their lives into building the Apostolic ministry over many years. They are strong in governmental structure, relationship and fathering of the next generation. There are also those who are what I call strategists. They haven't got the years of experience in fathering or building, but they do have a present day truth of strategy in building an effective apostolic network and organizing the spiritual warfare teams that are needed.

This pattern is seen in Elijah and Elisha in the Old Testament. Wherever Elijah went, Elisha made a choice to follow. When the mantle fell, he picked it up.

There is a time coming in the very near future that the government of God worldwide will be established. This will be like the New Testament "Jerusalem council" in its function. The Jerusalem council had three main tasks and mandates.

1. They extended the right hand of fellowship to Paul. By this they were acknowledging his apostolic ministry.

2. They set guidelines when asked. It's important to note the "when asked" part. They didn't run out to tell Paul how to do his ministry, they responded by request.

3. They were agents of change. They were instrumental in the transition of society from the Old Testament law to the age of grace.

I believe we will one day have Jerusalem councils with the same mandates and functions in our cities, across our nation and even one with an international perspective. I believe there will be Apostles with a call to the Jews, some to the Arab nations, some to China, some to India and so on.

When this government of God is established, it will release the signs and wonders of the Apostles where healing and miracles will be normal in the Sunday service of the local church.

The strategists have to assist the Apostolic fathers in developing the government structure before the strategies can be implemented. If the strategists go ahead of government, we will end up with another version of denominational structure. It would have strategy, but lack the governmental spiritual authority. It would have some success, but not the fullness of the power and presence of God.

If the Elijah's or the spiritual fathers ignore the Elisha strategists there will be a united government, but it will lack in strategic warfare. We are on the verge of a shift from the Prophetic to the strategic flow of God. This isn't to eliminate the prophetic, but rather, it's to release it! We are like a plane on a runway picking up speed, trying to take off. We are gaining momentum but we still tend to return back to the prophetic rather than the strategic. But with the momentum the take-off will be very soon.

There will come a time in our very near future that a Jerusalem council type Apostolic governmental team will get established. We hear about one-world governments in the natural but I believe it is also a spiritual principle. We will see Apostles from major geographical locations as well as those to spheres of authority in various people groups. These men and women (yes, women!) of God will be received and function in an international covering and accountability role as did the Jerusalem council of Paul's day. This will bring order, strategies and spiritual power to the Body of Christ that will shake the world!

There will be a spiritual governmental structure for regions of the earth. There will be governments over nations and a government over all the earth! **One world government!**

Each region of the earth will have a governmental team with a senior elder or Apostle of the team. That means that in international kingdom government there will be a recognized and received senior elder (Apostle). This person will be like President Bush of the United States. He (or she) will rally the troops, identify and seek out the enemy and build international relationship support against a common enemy! He will build and give direction to the government of God that will defeat "spiritual terrorism." This isn't somewhere in our distant future! Last year, at a conference I was at, the Lord gave me a revelation and a word for one of our great authors, a Pastor and leader in the Body of Christ. I believe he will be the one to rise to the call and lead the way to international governmental authority and the Kingdom of God being established upon the earth.

During this process I have been asking God for the redemptive purpose for Italy and specifically Rome. We have some indications in what has been said about them over years like, "all roads lead to Rome." My intercessors said they believed Rome was to be the steering wheel. We have seen in secular materials that Rome was the center of culture, music and arts. As I read the description it reminded me of the Davidic anointing being described in secular wording. I also believe it will have the essence of what Paul said in **Romans 1:8**...

> *First, I thank my God through Jesus Christ for you all, that <u>your faith is spoken of throughout the whole world</u>.*

It still is! But one day it will be a testimony of the born-again message it was when Paul wrote this letter!

As the apostolic network establishes the Government of God and picks up the mantle left by the Apostle Paul, I believe it will release the reality of New Testament Apostolic ministry with full signs and wonders.

There are two dimensions of effecting change. One is in the jurisdictional authority over a city or region that gives us authority to effect change in the heavenlies. The other is the power of influence.

There are places we have jurisdictional authority, and when we speak or prophecy in those places it has the "power to effect change" and establish order in the heavenlies. When we are in other places that we don't have the same jurisdictional authority, we still have the power of influence as we teach and preach to help those who do have the jurisdictional authority.

There appears to be a dilemma with this principle. We see the authority we have in parts of the country or regions of the world and yet we seem to be ineffective—or at least it appears to not have the same impact—at home as when we are overseas, etc. Many write this off to the statement Jesus made about a prophet being without honor in his own home.

I believe, that just as the local church is boot camp for the people, there is a spiritual "boot camp" called "community" God is using to train the Apostolic ministries for a city, region or nation.

With this in mind, I would like to make this statement! **"You aren't changing your community, your community is changing you!"**

You aren't developing your ministry, your ministry that God placed in you before you were born is developing you!

As you rise to apostolic leadership in your community it produces change in you. As you change, it releases a personal spiritual supremacy that gives you a new spiritual authority, and with the voice of authority in the spirit realm, combined with the power of influence in the natural you "effect change" in your community. And so, your community changes with you!

The results we see when we travel elsewhere are due to the boot camp principle. We are not the ones being trained by God when we travel. It isn't our region we are fighting. It isn't the spiritual stronghold we are called to tear down we are facing.

We are in another man's sphere and our anointing gets added to the spiritual power of those who are already there and have a call to that city or region. To them, this city is their boot camp and they will experience the same resistance and challenges personally and corporately as you do in your boot camp. You are there adding strength to strength so it has breakthrough power without much effort on your part!

The changes that happen in you and the growth you experience comes from facing the challenges at home in your city boot camp! If you are where the Lord has called you to be, then you are being trained by God and prepared to help others tear down specific strongholds and walk in a definable spiritual role in the Body in some areas by authority, in other areas by influence.

I want to bring this thought down to the local church level to describe it in more detail. Every principle we establish should apply to every dimension. The same principles we apply to the nations should work for our cities. They should work for the local church or for the family and can even be applied to the individual Christian experience.

Lets go back to boot camp and see how it works!

The layered anointing

One of the ways we see the fire of God fall is by the corporate anointing working in our services. I call this "the layered corporate anointing."

I watched a video from a church recently that is experiencing a strong presence of God. In that service I saw the worship leader build the faith of the people and focus their hearts on God. This created an atmosphere for God to work. In due time a visiting evangelist stepped in and gave an almost harsh instruction to repent. The people responded and the whole service was lifted to another level of intensity. Then the worship continued at the new level. After due time the senior Pastor stepped in and prophesied over the congregation of hope, confidence and blessings of God's presence. This again lifted the service to another level. (One anointing layered upon another). The worship continued again at a new level until a prophetic song special filled the air with another anointing and the result was a throne room atmosphere of God that the people couldn't ignore.

There was repentance, life-changing experiences and a reality of God released to the people. When the Word came, the people felt like they had been transported supernaturally from a church building into the presence of God Himself. I've heard people describe the experience as a feeling like thick air settled around them when the glory fell!

I believe this was accomplished by layered anointings working together adding weight to the canopy of God until it touched earth!

We have tried to get this kind of experience for years by using the superstars of song and skills. That's what King Saul was—a head and shoulders above everyone else. He stood out in the crowd. But the presence of God isn't coming through the Saul's or the superstars of gifts and talents, it's coming through the David's! Those that have a heart after God! Mighty men and women of God equipped for battle! Those who will take their place in the army of the Lord adding their strength and gifting to the team, walking in loyalty and unity with the leadership and the vision.

Momentum is maintained by layered anointing

Every service has the principle of following the fire of the Holy Spirit and watching for the mantle to fall, then picking up the mantle and using it. It may be that a healing anointing would fall in a service or a prophetic one or whatever the Lord may want to do. Follow the fire, see the mantle that falls and pick it up!

When we have special ministries come to our churches we can sometimes do ourselves more harm than good. I believe that the ministries that we invite should be compatible to our motivational identification and our ministry dynamics. What I mean by this is if, for instance, my church was based on cell groups and teaching and an evangelist stirs the church in another direction, it hasn't really helped me. If my ministry dynamic is teaching oriented rather than rallying the troops with energetic preaching, and we invite the evangelist to do crusades to gather the people for us, the people haven't come because of our gifting or our ministry dynamic. After the guest leaves and the church returns to our leadership, there is a contrast that gets noticed by the people. When this contrast shows up, we hear from the people, "When is that guest coming back again?"

We need to be able to grab the mantle that falls and use it! This takes teamwork.

When the special guest is there, we should be careful to still use the corporate team for the service. Many ministries I have had in the church aren't used to it; they are accustomed to being the focus of attention. But they are there for me and our church, not the other way around, so I do it anyway! They are there to deposit a spiritual blessing, not to add to their mailing list! I don't make them the total focus of the services because they aren't there next week, I am.

I organize the service so that two-thirds of the service momentum and dynamic is created with our team. The worship team still gets the same amount of time as they normally would. I watch for the fire of the Holy Spirit and wait for the mantle to fall.

In order for a new mantle to fall the guest needs to have a higher-level ministry than you already have or a special ministry anointing to impart. If they don't, why are they there?

Watch for the mantle to fall in the service and step into it **with the guest** to receive the impartation. (When Saul was with the Prophets, he prophesied!) Your real challenge as a leader is to grab that mantle and use it the next Sunday to do the same as the guest did. It's like a relay race. The baton gets passed to you to continue the journey. If you drop it or don't even try to grab it, the people will see it and you will be viewed in contrast as a lesser minister than the guest that came. This hurts your credibility in the eyes of the people, your momentum is lost and the people just go into neutral, waiting for the next crusade or the next event, hoping that God will show up.

When you use your team to carry the majority of the momentum in a service, the next Sunday two-thirds of the ministry dynamic or the atmosphere can be easily reproduced or re-established because it was they that did it in the first place.

The Pastor's real work isn't during the crusade or special Sunday, it's the Sunday that follows the crusade. Take the mantle that fell and use it with every effort you have. If the service has an atmosphere of expectation and a new dynamic to it, you have successfully received an impartation and the church goes to a new level. The people will also see you, the Pastor, at a new ministry level because you are now doing what the guests did. So they will lift you up as an equal to the guests rather than seeing a contrast that sets you lower in their eyes.

Layered corporate anointing can help you to successfully accomplish this process and move the church to a new level. All success and failure should be a corporate effort. We either make it together or we don't make it at all!

There are many aspects of the layered anointing but I think you get the idea. The anointings that God rises up in the local church "boot camp" are intended to be released beyond the four walls of the church.

There are many reasons they don't make it, but I want to address one of the very common ones I call **the Apostolic bottleneck**.

13

Apostolic Bottlenecks

There isn't any one person or one ministry that is taking their city alone.

A person that tries to do it alone or that rises up servants instead of sons and daughters will eventually become a pastoral or an apostolic bottleneck!

What I am referring to is a person who has to be at the top. One who feels threatened by strong leaders around them. Leaders that want the attention and credit for themselves. This type of leader won't release the fullness of the team potential.

The only dimension of the team effort that will get released is how much that leader can comprehend or teach or lead, instead of the combined body ministry of each part working in harmony releasing a far greater presence and power of God.

Every person in a church or every church in an organization should be identifiable as part of the greater body. This may be more in philosophy of ministry than expression. I think of it this way. You can touch the leg of an elephant and know its uniqueness, but still know it's part of the greater body. It has enough of the characteristics of the rest of the body to be identifiable as belonging to that body.

We are called to train and equip the saints for the work of the ministry. This means **rising up leaders and training teams to accomplish tasks**. If it has to be me in the spotlight, *I've become a bottleneck* or a restricting entity to the release of the fullness of the body ministry potential. The purpose of apostolic ministry isn't to build servants, but to train sons and daughters to do the work of the ministry. The goal is that **they will go higher and farther** than the one who mentored them. If they don't there are only two possibilities: one - they didn't try; or two - there was a bottleneck that restricted them from becoming all they should have become and kept them as servants of obedience rather than sons of maturity.

An apostolic leader needs to look up and down as they lead their team. A tendency is to be looking out to higher-level ministries for the new anointing or the fresh revelations and miss the ones that are right there in their own team or in their own church.

We tend to overlook the David's in our midst!

God speaks to many people who get missed if we aren't listening in the right direction. The keys to breakthrough in our particular region came from a man who had been caught up in witchcraft for twenty-five years. When he was saved and heard about the research we had done and revelations we had received, he knew what we were looking for. He had the knowledge we needed to find and confirm the violations and to Pastor our city. It unlocked the redemptive purpose as well as identified the strongholds.

Our pride, thinking he was a new Christian, or not at

a high level of spiritual understanding in the Lord, could have caused us to ignore him and we could have missed a great blessing. He had a Saul to Paul conversion and is one of the most loved men in our church! He had a shepherd's heart and wanted to care for the sheep. But he had a destiny in God and the keys for our city. He was a nobody like David, but a nobody with a destiny! **There are David's in our midst!**

Don't be blinded by pride! They have been placed in your "boot camp" for a reason! They have weapons of war or knowledge you will need to become all you are to be.

System norms

The successes of the layered anointing and corporate team building dynamics causes the body to edify or build itself up. As the body grows the leadership dynamic has to grow with it. New procedures are needed. I call these procedures **the system norms!**

A corporate team dynamic is different from a "mom and pop" organization. When the family business (or church) is small, mom and pop can keep their hands on everything that happens. When it grows to a size where it's impossible to do it all ourselves we need to change our leadership focus from "leading people" to "managing leaders."

As the corporate team is established, it's important that the dynamic of the team and the decision making process remains consistent, using the same system norms whether the manager, founder or senior Pastor is there or not. We tend to lead strong when we are there, making the decisions as we need to and changing them on the way down the hall if we have to. Then we leave and we expect the team to be able to carry it when we are gone. The problem usually is that if they don't get to make decisions when the senior Pastor is there, they won't know what to do when he's not. We hear many times about leaders who start to travel out from their church. They say things like, "When I return the wheelbarrow is still in the same place but now it's full of garbage." This isn't a sign of rebellious people, however, it's a sign of the leadership dynamic being used.

If we want a corporate team that is able to make right decisions, we have to empower them even when we are there. We establish direction with input from the team. We establish system norms for seasons of time to accomplish tasks by input from all involved. This is a win-win situation. It gives the team ownership and involvement at the same time as allowing them to give valued input that helps us avoid mistakes or unseen obstacles.

Changes to the system norms also have to be corporate. This affects the order of "people to see" as well as the "procedures to follow" under normal circumstances.

There are many times when we have to make a change because of an unforeseen circumstance, but we should still inform and involve the corporate team. What tends to happen is that the team makes a decision, develops a plan and sets out to fulfill it. Then the leader thinks about it and decides that it needs adjusting, and because he or she has been used to a mom and pop leadership dynamic instead of a corporate process, he or she will tend to make "on the spot" changes. The problem then becomes that everyone else is still heading the way they decided at the meeting, not knowing anything has changed. This can go unnoticed for long periods of time. If it happens too often it undermines the value of having a corporate team in the first place. Everyone will start to assume things will get changed anyway or that the leader will just do whatever he or she wants. This leads to team members feeling that following the system norm is just a waste of time, since they may as well just agree with the leader in the first place.

We all have the same desire. We want to bring the presence of God to our churches in a very real and experiential way. We can see in the Bible that the Lord wants to be with His people. We see how David brought back the ark in 2 Samuel 5.

We focus on David, but in reality he couldn't move the ark alone! **It took a team to move it!**

Moving the ark takes teamwork

The ark represented the presence of God with His people. We are always trying to build new ways or systems or programs that will bring His presence to us.

> *So they set the ark of God on a new cart, and brought it out of the house of Abinadab, which was on the hill; and Uzzah and Ahio, the sons of Abinadab, drove the new cart.*

> *2 Samuel 6:3*

David did what I think we are still doing today—he built a new cart. We are constantly trying to find the new way or the new fad that will bring the presence of God. But, we also find that we have about the same success as David did.

He did the right thing when he failed, he asked the Lord!

> **David was afraid of the LORD that day; and he said, "How can the ark of the LORD come to me?"**
>
> **2 Samuel 6:9**

When he asked the Lord he found the way that God had designed in the first place, and when he followed God's instructions the ark or the presence of God returned to His people.

Moving the
Ark of God

I believe moving the ark is a corporate effort.

The Bible shows in Numbers 2:9 that the tribe of Judah went first when the army was on the move. Judah means the 'praisers' and 'celebrators.' We know that the Lord inhabits the praises of His people. When the praise goes forth first, God's presence has breakthrough power. We see an example in Acts 16 as Paul and Silas sang and the presence of God came and they were freed from prison.

The first thing that we lose when an attack of the enemy comes is our ability (or really it's the desire) to praise the Lord. If the devil can stop us from praising, we don't bring in His presence.

A church that is on the move will recognize this next principle clearly. I watch our worship team like a hawk. If the praisers and celebrators are out front, then they are the first ones to confront a new stronghold of the enemy. (Remember, we are not the ones who have built a stronghold or a fortress to hide in. We are the invading army of the Lord!)

The new battles and strategies of the devil can be seen first in them. They are like the initial strike force, the first tactical team to land on the beach!

They are the first to encounter the enemy's stronghold! If you watch the music teams for any dynamic changes, personal conflicts or division, you will see the new battle you are entering into and be able to defeat it within the worship team before it gets into the church.

So, the first principle of moving the ark is an attitude of praise and celebration.

> *So it was, when Joshua had spoken to the people, that the seven priests bearing the seven trumpets of rams' horns before the LORD advanced and blew the trumpets, and the ark of the covenant of the LORD followed them. The armed men went before the priests who blew the trumpets, and the rear guard came after the ark, while the priests continued blowing the trumpets.*
>
> *Joshua 6:8-9*

> *Then seven priests bearing seven trumpets of rams' horns before the ark of the LORD went on continually and blew with the trumpets. And the armed men went before them. But the rear guard came after the ark of the LORD, while the priests continued blowing the trumpets.*
>
> *Joshua 6:13*

The first leaders in the order of this Scripture were those who were armed for war, who went before the priests who were blowing the trumpets.

The evangelists are the ones who I believe are equipped for signs and wonders and a boldness in God! They have a warfare gifting to go into a new land with power.

The next ones are those who blew the trumpets. They are the prophetic ones who can see into the distance and proclaim words of confirmation and warnings of dangers on the journey. They stir the faith of the people with the word of the Lord. They bring words of encouragement and vision.

The ark itself is carried by poles, which are held at the four corners. These four corners are:

1. Worship

2. Prayer

3. Fellowship

4. Teaching of the Word

All churches need to have these elements in place to move forward in God.

The poles that hold the ark are poles of administration.

"We need to be apostolic in nature but administrational in practice."

The rear guard are those who follow the ark. They are with the people making sure the needs are met, that the people continue to walk and that nobody gets left behind. These are the Pastors of the body, those that love and care for those that follow the ark. They provide encouragement, love, food and shelter, hope and direction for everyone who follows.

The apostolic government is placed on the shoulders of them all. That means someone had the gifting to train and equip the prophets, evangelists, pastors and teachers for the work of the ministry. They had the ability to unite them in vision and direction. They gave them ownership of the purpose and built teamwork within the people. These are the Apostles of God.

With this structure in place I see praise with breakthrough power, evangelists that work miracles, prophets that are accurate and complete, worship with reverence, prayer with power, fellowship with love, and the word that inspires!

The pastors will have their hands full ministering to all the new people that join the journey to the Promised Land! This is the corporate anointing!

The corporate team at the front line of Battle is a protection and a strength.

We tend to think that as the glory of God falls or as the church goes forward that the Pastor or key leaders are on the front line and everyone else is behind them. In reality, the front line of the canopy that settles down doesn't have just an arrowhead point on it. The front line runs the full width of the canopy and *anywhere the canopy of light touches and pushes back darkness it becomes a front line.* That means that every leader of a prayer team, youth ministry, Sunday school class, home group, worship team, or any other department of the church is on the front line sooner or later.

Every task needs a team, every team needs a leader. The formula we use is this:

"Identify the task, then train a leader to build a team to accomplish that task."

When we have individuals rather than teams, all the enemy needs to do is to take out that individual any way he can. When he succeeds it creates a hole in the front line that he can come through into the church.

This can happen physically, relationally or spiritually by things like offense. A corporate team at every level on the front line adds extra strength and power to the task, but it also protects the church. If someone on the team or the team leader himself falls for some reason, the corporate team stops the breach in the front line and keeps the enemy out of the church and maintains the strength until a new leader is established.

The devil can't stop us from going forward because the presence of God keeps breaking through. So he tries to come into the throne room with the saints and attack from behind. If the leader is going before God for the people, his back is exposed to the people. This is the weakest area of the Christian armor. The enemy has to find a way into the church to get to that weakness. The corporate or team strength of the church is both power and protection for the Pastor. They protect his back and guard the integrity of the church.

Covering—Onion Skin Layers

In the concept of Kingdom government there is a King. His Name is Jesus! He is the head of the church but the government shall rest upon His shoulders! The church!

His shoulders—the church—starts with government.

There are many government types. Just about every organization has a unique structure that they feel allows them to do what the Lord has called them to do. What I look for in the government of any organization is 1) Accountability; 2) Support when needed; 3) Relationship; 4) Definable structure.

We can have good administration and still not have relationship. Many of our Pastor friends have only the local ministerial to turn to for help or fellowship. In our particular situation, we have a relationship network of churches. It's mandatory that every Pastor has a Pastor who speaks into his life. This is done by establishing a tangible ongoing relationship. This relationship is long-term even if the geographical situations change.

The Pastor's Pastor has to be someone who is more seasoned or able to pour into his life. I like to think of it as having two glasses, one full of water, and one empty. If they are set on a table side by side there isn't any way to pour the water from the full one into the empty one. In order to pour into the empty one we have to lift the full one higher so the water can be poured down. It's the same in the spirit realm; we need to be willing to receive from those who rule over us or are above us in the Lord.

"If we see ourselves as equals we can't receive".

I see it in the body all the time. Anybody that starts to lower the Pastor down to being just a friend or "one of the boys" will begin to see him as an equal. The first noticeable thing that happens is he drops the Pastor title and goes to a first name basis.

Most of the Pastors don't really care about titles, but

a title says something about how that person sees you. If you become an equal in his eyes instead of his covering, he has either brought you down or lifted himself up. In either case, his ability to receive from you has been neutralized or at least reduced.

This will show itself in its fullness as soon as you have to speak into his life or you do something he doesn't like. "You will drop one more notch from friend to enemy."

I never refer to my Pastor by his first name even when my wife (Kim) and I are alone or we are with him on the golf course or the beach. It's not for his benefit—it's for mine! When I get into troubles in my life I don't want the advice of a friend, I want my Pastor to get the wisdom of God and help me through. If I have lowered him in my eyes to being just a friend, then I won't receive what the Lord tells him if it's not what I want to hear.

My Pastor is my friend and I enjoy when we get to spend time together. The best way I can protect myself and strengthen my position for the days of trouble is by disciplining my mind with a constant reminder that I have someone to turn to for help or to correct me when it's needed. This is established by honoring the position I have asked him to take in my life by referring to him and about him as my Pastor.

We tend to wait for troubles before we establish relationship accountability in our lives. This isn't the way to win battles.

Asa...__built fortified cities__ in Judah, for the land had rest; he __had no war in those years__, because the LORD had given him rest.

2 Chronicles 14:6

During times of peace he fortified the city. That's a good illustration of how to get through a battle. The relationships you build during the times of peace *before the battles come* will determine your strength. If we don't have a relationship before troubles come, it will be too late to establish one. During the heat of battle it doesn't seem to matter who is invited into the situation to help, it just increases the intensity and there really never is an agreement on both sides that this was the right person. The relationship with outside accountability needs to established during times of peace so there isn't any question as to who will be called when troubles come.

Any organization could adapt a philosophy of relationship, accountability and support if they choose to. When we do, it places us in a much stronger position in the natural realm, but also in the spiritual. I call this the "onion skin layers" of covering. When I placed myself and our church under the covering of my Pastor it also placed us under his blessings. We became sons and daughters of the house. His battles became my battles, his blessings became my blessings.

Jesus referred to this principle in **Luke 22:28-30**.

> *But you are those who have continued with Me in My trials. And I bestow upon you a kingdom, just as My Father bestowed one upon Me, that you may eat and drink at My table in My kingdom, and sit on thrones judging the twelve tribes of Israel.*

I have an increased authority in the spirit realm because I am under authority. It goes past the authority and blessings of my Pastor because he also has a Pastor and covering over his life and church. This starts to show the onion skin layers of protection.

If the devil wants to attack me, he has to penetrate the layers that are over me. So the only way he really can get at me is:

1. If I remove myself from covering or...

2. If I allow division or relationship problems with those that rule over me, or even attitudes against them or...

3. Willful or knowledgeable sin.

This doesn't mean that I don't have an opinion or a say in my life, but even times of conflict can be navigated with a right attitude and with right actions.

If there is strife and division the enemy can penetrate the layers of protection through that opening and get right into my life.

So now I need to close that doorway by repentance or change. Then I can get rid of the devils that come in.

The same relationship principles apply to the inner structure or culture of the local church. Just as the Pastor needs to continue to strengthen his or her covering by relationship, every level of the church needs to do the same. In our attitudes and actions we need to be careful we aren't removing ourselves from covering by offenses that don't get dealt with or prideful attitudes that say "I know more than the Pastor anyway!" Knowledgeable sin opens a doorway for devils by exposing ourselves to the judgement of God against that sin. There isn't any covering that can protect us from these actions.

The Corporate Team

We would probably all agree that we should train up sons and daughters. It's our greatest achievement in a ministry lifetime to train and equip another generation to rise higher and go farther than we did. We continue this thought as we consider our own position as senior Pastors or leaders. Many have tried to raise up a spiritual son that has all the same giftings and abilities as we do.

We use the Elijah and Elisha, Moses and Joshua or Paul and Timothy approach to raising up the next generation. We know that to survive, they must be strong leaders able to run the church. The problem is, *if they are strong enough to run your church for you, they will!*

We see many great leaders that have entrusted their life's work to their well trained junior or associate as they go out to help other ministries in their troubles. What happens in many circumstances is that when the Pastor returns from helping others, the church has been taken over by the spiritual son and the senior no longer has a position or a role to play. After a lifetime of work, they are done.

As I stated earlier, the other side of the situation is when the senior leader holds onto so much control that nothing gets done when they leave. This can also be seen in another way when a Pastor moves on and no one has been trained to do what he did so the work slows or stops completely.

What do we do?

The success I have seen in the business world as well as in the church is based on corporate anointing or team building.

God has already prepared the next generation for teamwork. *They value relationship over achievement.* In my generation it was every man for himself. My friends were those who were heading the same direction and those who were task-oriented, doing the same things and achieving similar success. If someone had different interests or wasn't heading in the same direction as I was, I would lose interest in maintaining that relationship. This generation values their relationships with their friends above achievement in itself. They will sacrifice their ultimate achievement for stronger relationships. This is a good sign that we are being prepared for a relational government of God.

Jesus chose who He wanted on His team. We should note here that He gave the whole multitude the word or the vision. From those that responded to the vision, He chose twelve to be the leaders, or the government. In the twelve, He had three that were closer to Him. Of the three, He had one most beloved disciple.

"Team building is all about relationship."

If we want to have a work continue on or even get

stronger when the Lord opens more doors for us or we are not able to carry it on for any reason, *we need to be strong in team building.*

In the next section I want to address some of my thoughts on corporate team building dynamics. Corporate teams have incredible potential for strength and protection. Most of us have trouble building them due to insecurities, fears, past leaders that hurt us or many other legitimate reasons. These hurts and fears are real, but they don't remove the necessity of team building.

How do you build a team?

1. Know what you are trying to accomplish in vision and purpose. Identify the big picture or task.

If you are where you are supposed to be in the Lord and doing what He created you to do, you have all the gifts and abilities within you (or at least a strong knowledge of them) to accomplish the tasks. So you start building a team by identifying what you are trying to accomplish. This goes back to knowing your redemptive purpose and that of your church. God mobilized His people out of Egypt by vision but eventually had to display the fruit. We need to do both to lead the people. Cast the vision and display the fruit!

2. Break the tasks down into sections.

As soon as you know your redemptive purpose you will be able to identify what tasks need to be done in order to accomplish the purpose. Break the big picture down into individual tasks and write down each task.

When you are finished making a list of these tasks, create a chart with these tasks listed, placing them in a circle with you in the middle. This circle of tasks should describe a larger but more defined picture of you and your redemptive purpose before God.

We have used many models as we have trained leaders over the years. We began with the pyramid structure that had the leader at the top giving instruction and direction to the teams. The weakness of this structure was that we ended up with dictated programs enforced by rules and punishment for the offenders rather than relationships with a common purpose. In this structure and with this philosophy we would build programs, try to motivate people to run them and then ask the Lord to fill them. A better plan is to find out what the Lord is doing, and build a program that embraces it with leaders that have a passion for it.

We then moved to an inverted pyramid style of leadership that focused on servant leaders. It had more heart in it but eventually put all the burden to carry every ministry on the shoulders of the senior Pastor or organizational leader. We then went to a horizontal pyramid or arrow concept of taking the rod of authority and leading the people. This is also strong in vision but lacks in corporate ownership principles. We ended up with a group of followers instead of an army of leaders.

The circle with the team leader in the middle allows for individual ownership of each department with accountability and equipping principles being applied by the senior Pastor. This can be done by relationship with team leaders. The structure looks more like a pattern of the universe or a picture of a living cell than a corporate flow chart.

Each department of the church has a team leader and each team leader builds a team to accomplish the task. Each team works in harmony with the other teams that are related to that area of ministry. This structure gives them autonomy and direction-setting power for that department of the church. This gives them a sense of ownership and achievement that doesn't change when the senior Pastor isn't there.

The senior Pastor in the center of the corporate wheel structure has the responsibility to make all the departments function together as one, like the coach of a football team would do. They would keep their eyes on the goal, develop individual players, develop team strategies and hold each team player accountable to his or her area of responsibility.

Each team has a common purpose, philosophy and attitude about them that is common to all teams. The task is what varies, and the process to accomplish the task is where they have ownership.

3. Train leaders with the skills to accomplish each task. Find people who are better at the individual task than you are.

This is hard for some leaders because of insecurities or a sense of losing control. In reality it's totally the opposite. The leader of that individual task doesn't really want the responsibility or have the ability to run everything—their gifting and redemptive purpose isn't to manage a corporate team, it's to lead and be successful in their area of expertise. They rise up quickly and do a great job, better than you can in that specific area of responsibility.

I watch for leaders to rise up when the need is made known. I don't really want to appoint a task or ask someone to do it just because it needs to be done. I avoid that when I can. I try to just let the need be known and watch for who rises up to meet that need. I have been surprised many times at who steps forward. We look for the Saul's of life to do the tasks, but God chooses the David's that have the right heart towards the task, or, in other words, those who take ownership of it.

If people aren't rising up to help with the tasks it's a sign that:

    a. the vision or purpose isn't clear, or

    b. they don't believe it, or

    c. they lack confidence that you can actually lead them into it.

In the early days of our ministry our vision was big, but we had very few who would help. I used to say, "If people aren't laughing at your vision it isn't big enough!" Others didn't really know if we could do it or not so they were reluctant to commit to it at the beginning. Also, church people are used to seeing the Pastors leave after only a few years and they don't want to be left holding the bag or with a responsibility they can't carry. I asked one of my heroes of the faith, and he gave me this good advice.

"Just go there and see who follows. If only one follows, pour your life into that one and then reproduce it!"

If you start to do the tasks and fulfill the redemptive purpose yourself there will be fruit in it. When others see the fruit and your commitment, it's contagious and they to will rise to the challenge and take ownership of the vision.

4. Then I train them, using the five steps in our training program.

    a. Teach them the word and the principles they need

    b. Show them how to do it

    c. Do it with them

    d. Watch them do it

    e. Release them on their own.

I allow them to have ownership of the process. It's up to me as a leader to establish the target and to help define the reality of where we are starting from. We can't let go of the direction-setting or vision-casting process. The process of how to achieve that goal, however, can be given into the hands of the leader and his or her team to carry out, even though we still have to watch over the process to make sure it doesn't head the wrong direction or that it isn't stuck in a rut.

The team may wander from a straight line that you would have taken from your experience, but as long as they are making progress and not really in danger, it's important to let them continue to work it out. We have to let the team work together to solve the problems to accomplish the tasks even "if we could" step in and solve it for them quickly. They need to learn to become a self-motivated and self-correcting team.

We always have to keep in mind that the whole

value of the task in the first place isn't achievement—it's people, teamwork and leadership development. In reality, even if they fail they have still gained important knowledge and skills to use in the future for their life and ministry. They now have teamwork skills and experience to work with right from the beginning of a new task so their probability of success increases dramatically. After two or three tasks even a weaker team can learn by experience how to function in corporate team dynamics and successfully accomplish tasks. The philosophy of people over task gives a greater strength and reward over the long term.

5. Establish situations in the natural to check their motives.

Great leaders are servants by nature!

This great principle I watch for is found in **Luke 22:24-27.**

> *Now there was also a dispute among them, as to which of them should be considered the greatest. And He said to them, "The kings of the Gentiles exercise lordship over them, and those who exercise authority over them are called 'benefactors.' But not so among you; on the contrary, he who is greatest among you, let him be as the younger, and he who governs as he who serves. For who is greater, he who sits at the table, or he who serves? Is it not he who sits at the table? Yet I am among you <u>as the One who serves</u>.*

You will find that preaching vision will stir up

carnality! People will compete for position and recognition. Even in Jesus' day they wanted to know who could sit at His right hand or at His left. Many times we see this relationship tension and we think devils are at work. We see offenses in the team and a negative attitude towards other members. We think it's devils, but in reality it's human nature. The devils will use these things to cause troubles and doorways to work through, but the root cause is human nature. We can't cast out human nature any more than we can counsel a devil!

I like to preach the vision and keep it before the people on a regular basis, but I do see that when I focus on vision, carnality is stirred. It appears that the devil doing a work, but in reality it's only the doorway of carnality. If the door stays open the devil will come through, but initially you are only dealing with human nature. You can't cast out human nature, and you can't counsel a devil. Learning to distinguish between them is important when building teams.

When we provide opportunity it reveals the devils at work influencing the souls (attitudes) of potential leaders.

Many years ago I worked for my uncle in a radio and television sales and service shop. It was before the years of cable TV. Back then when the signal wasn't very strong we would install a signal booster on the incoming line to amplify the signal to the television. This did the job as the picture got brighter, but so did the lines of interference! The weaknesses in the signal also became easier to see!

It's the same with the anointing. When the Lord boosts the signal or increases the anointing in your life it amplifies your gifts and abilities but it also makes your weaknesses easier to see!

This is why I say that opportunity stirs the devils. It amplifies or reveals the influence of the demonic forces on our carnal nature.

I like to **test teachability with natural responsibility**. I watch for or create situations that test the potential leaders' attitudes and relationship towards myself, the team and the vision. Great leaders will always jump into the middle of the situation and serve the church or the team. If they don't have a servant's heart they will have a dictator mentality to those they try to lead. Great leaders are servants of all!

I assign tasks to them and give them ownership of the tasks to watch how they respond. If they become independent or prideful, or don't deal well with the other team members then I know what to do next. If they respond well, then I assign them greater responsibility and positions of more recognized influence to the people.

When they make mistakes I don't write them off. I have a system for that as well, called the mistake line.

The mistake line

I will work with anybody who is willing. Many times we let people serve until they make a mistake and that's where we put a ceiling on their growth and development. I let these mistakes be a foundation or a starting point of training rather than a ceiling.

Not many people are bad at everything! Everyone has a reason he or she exists and why the Lord has added them to His church. So our job is to unlock the redemptive purpose and give them skills to accomplish tasks and help them fit into the corporate team. The things they do well will continue to grow if you give them opportunity.

The weak areas are where I put my time. The goal is to lift that area of weakness up to a new level so they can do more intense ministry and carry more responsibility before their skills or experience causes them to make mistakes.

The point is that we shouldn't let honest mistakes eliminate them from serving. *If they are teachable they will learn.*

I always say *"if you aren't making any mistakes you aren't trying hard enough."* If you are trying as hard as you can and stretching your experience you will make mistakes. **Don't be afraid of mistakes.** Use them to learn from and go forward in faith. The key to success is getting up one more time than you have fallen down.

All great men and women who rose to do great things have made mistakes, said and did things that hurt people unintentionally, or missed the leading of God and had to go back and start again. They just had enough determination to try again. My dad used to say the only failure there is "is not trying!" When we try, like Peter stepping out of the boat, and fail, we have still learned something that we can use to try again, so we really haven't lost at all.

Another great principle is seen in **Luke 22:28-30**.

> **But you are those who have continued with Me in My trials. And _I bestow upon you a kingdom, just as My Father bestowed one upon Me_, that you may eat and drink at My**

table in My kingdom, and sit on thrones judging the twelve tribes of Israel.

6. This principle is called Impartation.

When we serve someone more seasoned in ministry we enjoy the privilege of sitting at the banqueting table with him or her. This means going with them as they minister and having people or churches open their hearts of relationship and give opportunity for ministry because they know your spiritual covering or your spiritual parents. You are seen as their family, so you are received on their reputation. This gives you favor in places that would take years to earn on your own. It's eating at your father's banqueting table. It took him or her years to establish, but you get to enjoy it by invitation. I believe the greatest apostolic principle is in impartation. What took your spiritual father or mother thirty years to establish can be imparted to you in five. They had to learn by trial and error. We learn from impartation.

It also allows you to grow with that ministry and develop your own skills as you serve. This gives you a chance to learn and to prove your abilities. When the need for leadership arises you get the opportunity and receive your own kingdom or your own responsibilities before God, just as Paul would send Timothy as a faithful son.

Impartation is done by relationship.

We need to have the determination of Elisha in **2 Kings 2:2**.

Then Elijah said to Elisha, "Stay here, please,

for the LORD has sent me on to Bethel." But Elisha said, "As the LORD lives, and as your soul lives, I will not leave you!" So they went down to Bethel.

We need to have the determination to follow someone we want an impartation from. "If you're going, I'm going!"

At the same time, the one who is doing the mentoring has to be willing to allow another person into their personal life. We can't just spend work time together, we need to also spend social time and travel time and get involved in very personal ways.

Mentoring from a distance will raise up servants, but close relationship mentoring will raise up sons and daughters who have received an impartation of our anointing that gets added to their anointing. This in itself can become a double portion anointing because my own abilities before God have been released and my spiritual father's anointing has been imparted. Now I can function in both.

7. Identify strengths and weaknesses.

The strengths that the Lord has placed in someone's life are usually quite easy to see. These strengths I have called your **"Breakthrough Anointing!"**

I referred to Jeremiah 1 earlier where we can see that the Lord had placed a purpose and a call on his life even before he was born. With the call comes the anointing or the special gifts and strengths to fulfill that call. We all have these special abilities that are unique to our redemptive purpose. We need to help people (especially potential leaders) define and exercise their breakthrough anointing. This will give them a great ability to overcome many of the emotional issues we try to counsel.

It's important to know your own breakthrough anointing because if you are Pastoral in gifting and try to use an evangelistic focus to encourage yourself or stir your faith it will be like Saul's armor was to David. It won't fit! You won't be able to fight and win! You need to use the one that is relative to your gifting.

We can identify a leader's "breakthrough anointing," but the real key to their success is found in identifying and overcoming their weaknesses. The devil knows he can't win against the anointing. The Bible says **the anointing breaks the yoke!** He can't contain it—it keeps breaking out! So he will attack the areas of weakness.

Any person rising to leadership in the body of Christ will be tested in their areas of weakness. They can't be hidden because God will continue to expose them. He doesn't do this to be mean or to cause church problems. He does it in answer to our prayers for Him to use us and allow us to rise into the fullness of our ministry. If someone struggles with rejection and the Lord doesn't bring healing and victory over it, all the devil has to do the first time that new leader is going to pray for someone or do an altar call, is to stir someone to say something like, "Who do you think you are?" or "What are you doing here? You aren't any good!" The weakness or sensitivity to rejection would stop that minister from any good he or she would have done. So the Lord continues to expose these weaknesses in the church "boot camp" so He can remove any weapons the devil could use against us. The areas of weakness then get filled with the presence and strength of God and become a great strength so they, too, can say like Paul did, **"In my weakness I have become strong!"**

    a. When you preach vision it stirs carnality, but carnality can be overcome by mentoring and teaching.

    b. Opportunity, on the other hand, will reveal devils at work and the devil's influence on our carnal nature. This exposes the weakness of the potential leader. The doorways have to be closed and this may even take deliverance to overcome.

8. Determine their ministry dynamics.

Are they bold and outspoken? Are they reserved and quiet? Are they more comfortable in front of a large group stirring up the crowd or in a home group with intimacy and relationship?

Our ministry dynamics are important. There is nothing worse than trying to fill a position that doesn't suit our personality and ministry dynamic. When we are passive by nature and try to use the techniques of a bold and outspoken visionary it comes across like Saul's armor and it offends the people rather than inspires them. It's not the message that offends them; it's the messenger's presentation that doesn't come across as sincere because it's obviously not his or her natural ministry dynamic.

9. Determine their motivational identification.

This is simply put as "What gets them out of bed in the morning?" or "What would they be doing even if they didn't get paid for it?"

People who are called to pray never need to be motivated to pray. They don't have to be reminded that there is a prayer meeting at the church. They are self-motivated because they want to be there. The same is for musicians or teachers or Prophets of God. People will be attracted to others of like faith.

We need to match the leaders with tasks that tap into their self-motivated interests and then they will feel a sense of accomplishment and purpose as they carry it out.

We tend to identify the tasks or build a program and then appoint or look for leaders who are willing to run that department. I say we should turn it the other way around. Find the leader and determine what motivates him or her and then *build the task around that self-motivated gifting.*

We might think that we wouldn't get enough leaders to run our departments that way, but I say *if God isn't rising up a leader, do we really need the program?*

We may be able to tell what is important to the Lord by simply watching whom He raises up to help!

10. Another very important issue is their philosophy of ministry.

I find that I have more discussions with potential leaders about philosophy of ministry or applied theology than I do about theology itself. We can have the same written statements of faith and theology but still apply it in totally different ways.

Many organizations could trade theological documents with another organization and not really affect anything too much. Trading the philosophy of ministry or the way that theology is applied, on the other hand, would change everything about them.

This shows up the most in the way we approach discipline. When someone makes a mistake there are many views of what should be done and how harsh we should be. The two trains of thought are these: 1) law and consequence, or 2) grace.

There are leaders that believe that rules are made to enforce. If you break a rule there is an immediate consequence. Other leaders put restoration and the long-term well being of the individual ahead of the short-term correction.

I like to minister by grace. Grace doesn't mean the absence of rules or the absence of consequences. **It does mean, however, that the one doing the correcting is also taking the responsibility for the long-term development of the one who made a mistake.**

We are so worried about our reputations and the appearance that there are only perfect people in our church that we want the problem to go away quickly. So we tend to take the easy route or the shortcut and just establish consequences to wrong actions.

A young person who gets expelled from school for not treating a teacher right probably has rejection already working in them and when we expel them it only re-enforces the root problem.

I do believe there are actions and consequences to poor behavior, but the way we approach it should be with an intention to do all we can to restore the relationship, build the character of the individual and keep them part of the corporate body for continued positive influence into their lives.

I like to say to my leaders, "If you aren't willing to do

the long-term work of cleaning, don't point out the dirt!"

Or..."Don't go around telling people what they are doing wrong unless you are willing to do all you can to help them do it right!"

God has revealed their faults and mistakes to you or put you into this situation for a reason. You can build or you can tear down. You can get the revenge by consequences or you can develop a long-term strategy of love, teaching and encouragement.

If a person of any age sees that you are willing to walk with them as they learn, they may not like the consequences of what they did, but they will appreciate the support they get from you to learn from this experience so they can avoid troubles in their future.

11. Talk to them about their vision—short and long term.

Many times we bring into our leadership teams people who don't plan to stay around for very long. We put them into key positions because they are gifted with people or talented in some way we hope will give us a boost. The problem is that they don't have the same long-term principles working in them that we do.

Build your core leadership team with those who have long-term vision for your church. The ones that come for a short term can still have effective and important roles to play, but they should be in support roles to the long-term team members. This adds stability to the team and an increased confidence in the leadership team from the people. The principle is this: short-term people should always serve long-term people regardless of how gifted they are.

12. Determine their power of influence.

There are those who have natural leadership abilities and powers of influence that other people just follow. Our leaders need to have relationship abilities and the needed skills to do the job, but a greater factor to watch for is the power of influence. I heard a preacher say, "If you think you are a leader, here's a test—look behind you, and if there isn't anyone following, you're just out for a walk!" I would rather have a leader with less skill but an ability to influence than a leader with great skill but no influence.

People won't follow some leaders no matter how good of a project they appear to be promoting. If you choose a leader that has both ability and influence all you have to do is keep that leader on track and others will follow.

Watch for bell heifers. This is a cowboy term. While herding cattle there are heifers that tend to wander away from the herd. When they do, others tend to follow them. Some wise cowboys determined that if they kept these wandering heifers going in the direction they should go, the rest would follow, so they hung bells around their necks to identify them.

Every workplace and church has people who are bell heifers. If they are going the direction you want to go the rest will follow. They don't need to have a title to be a bell heifer. They just have influence and people tend to follow their lead no matter what direction they take. Good leaders are good leaders, but bell heifers will lead people in directions of blessings or curses, whether they are good or bad, and go where they want—not necessarily where you want them to go. Identify who they are and spend time getting them headed in the same direction as you are and they will become a great asset to the body. Ignore them and many will stray. Don't depend on the strength of your projects alone to keep people on track. Influence is a powerful force.

13. Watch for those who have taken ownership.

I always say that if you want to find out who is a leader, throw a problem out there and see who jumps into the middle to solve it. **"True leaders are birthed in times of troubles."** If people around you go into neutral when troubles come and won't take a stand on one side or another, they aren't the long-term leaders you want with you. I would rather have a person who took a stand against me in an issue but later was won over or convinced me I was wrong, than have one that stayed neutral and didn't have a clear position in the situation at all.

I listen to the terminology of people all the time. When I am talking to them and they are saying what is needed in "your church," I know they haven't taken ownership of it or else they would be saying "our church."

It's the same with vision or troubles. If it is "your" trouble, "our" trouble or "my" trouble it reveals a varying degree of ownership. As long as it is "yours" and not "ours" there isn't any hope of them staying with you when the things get rough.

14. The 80/20principle.

I've heard Pastors and leaders say for years that 20% of the people will take up 80% of your time. This is true if you're the only one doing the ministry. When you function in corporate dynamic you can resolve this situation by delegation.

I let 20% take up my time, but they are the top 20% productive leaders around me. As I spend time with them they grow and become more able to help others.

Look at how fast it multiplies. Alone, I can only deal with about six to eight people per week with in-depth or time-consuming ministry problems. If my wife works with me we can actually do the work of three, so it increases to maybe twelve to eighteen people per week. But if I train leaders that can look after and mentor other leaders I can effectively and relationally train at least twelve like Jesus did.

When I put my time into them and they minister to the people, I can now look after 6 people x 12 disciples = 72 people each week without working harder myself.

This scenario is illustrating people who are having major time-consuming problems, not the bigger picture of evangelism. I can look after 75 to 100 people by relationship easily if they are having a normal amount of troubles in their lives. With a team of twelve it multiplies to between 1000 and 1200 people who can be Pastored.

When we take it to the next generation of leaders where each leader trains another twelve, the numbers are amazing. So, to put this into perspective, if it takes ten years to train twelve good, solid leaders that can train other leaders, I may only have those twelve leaders and their families in my church because most of my efforts are focused on them. But through that time they start to mentor and train another generation of leaders. I don't mean by age, as though they were waiting for the younger ones to be old enough. I mean new people that get saved and join the church. If each one mentored twelve we would have 144 leaders plus their families in ten years and so on. It shows the incredible potential of training leaders and building teams to accomplish tasks.

It benefits everyone to focus on training.

15. Include them in your personal life (as friends)

Recognition and thanks are important principles of team building, but this is even more beneficial. I try to spend more time with my leaders as friends than in doing task-oriented activities. (Asa fortified the cities during times of peace!)

This is hard for someone who is a task-oriented visionary. It doesn't come naturally, so I have to treat it as a learned behavior and a discipline in my life.

Our common goals and vision can do a lot when troubles come, but **the real glue** to hold a team together is based on the strength of the relationships outside of the task.

Take the "TRIP" together!

Any team is held together by principles. I want to give you four that I believe are needed. This applies internally for the local church or corporately in any size organization.

   a. Theology: To have a functioning strong team we need to be theologically compatible.

   b. Relationship: We must be relationship-based and team oriented in dynamic. Our organizational strategies of meetings and fellowship must show and practically build relationship strength. If all we do is talk business we can be strong in administration but still weak in relationship. We have to strategically build relationships that work.

c. Identity: There is great power to effect change as a corporate identity is built. The hippies of the 60'and 70's had cultural identities and common values that had enough power to effect change in corporate America. We need to maintain our uniqueness, but there are still many ways we can be recognized as part of the larger corporate entity.

d. Philosophy: The way we do things or the way we apply our knowledge of scripture is as important as knowing the scripture itself.

All four of these principles need to be identified and maintained to have long-term relationships that can go through almost any kind of trials and still last.

The most important principle is a given, and I would assume that you already know and practice it— PRAYER. We need to constantly ask the Holy Spirit for His guidance in choosing leaders and only respond when it seems good to us and the Holy Spirit!

The Three Strongholds We Face

The three main powers or spirits I believe we are dealing with in the spirit realm are:

1. The spirit of Leviathan or the devil himself.

2. The spirit of strife that robs the harvest by creating 2 camps.

3. The spirit of rebellion that works like witchcraft.

All of these work through the doorway of our carnal "attitude" or "spirit" of error, when we make decisions with our hearts like Saul or others before us did instead of just remaining faithful to the instructions of God! The influence of Leviathan on our soul is seen in what we call our carnal nature.

The realm of our warfare isn't with people. We don't need to fight with people to win a battle or to fulfill the redemptive purpose of God.

For we do not wrestle against flesh and blood, but against principalities, against powers, against the rulers of the darkness of this age,

against spiritual hosts of wickedness in the heavenly places.

Ephesians 6:12

Our battle is a spiritual one! There are those who say we are at peace, but the Bible tells us to put on the full armor of God. You don't put on armor to go to the beach or to go on a vacation. We put on armor to be ready for battle!

The doorway is opened by an attitude of error.

I want to break this down and define what I mean by it. The Bible shows the "attitude" of error in many places. The first one I want to draw attention to is in **1 Samuel 1:3**...

This man went up from his city yearly to worship and sacrifice to the LORD of hosts in Shiloh. Also the two sons of Eli, Hophni and Phinehas, <u>the priests of the LORD</u>, were there.

Eli's two sons where the priests who looked after the tabernacle of the Lord. But look at **1 Samuel 2:12...**

Now the sons of Eli <u>were corrupt; they did not know the LORD</u>. (V:17) Therefore the sin of the young men was very great before the LORD.

The Bible goes on to show that Eli was aware of the problem.

Now Eli was very old; and <u>he heard everything his sons did</u> to all Israel, and how they lay with the women who assembled at *the door of the tabernacle of meeting.*

1 Samuel 2:22

He spoke to his sons but they didn't listen. The corruption continued until one day the Lord sent a Prophet with a word....

Why do you kick at My sacrifice and My offering which I have commanded in My dwelling place, and honor your sons more than Me [the judgement of God came] Therefore the LORD God of Israel says: 'I said indeed that your house and the house of your father would walk before Me forever.' But now the LORD says: 'Far be it from Me; for those who honor Me I will honor, and those who despise Me shall be lightly esteemed.'

1 Samuel 2:29-30

Now this shall be a sign to you that will come upon your two sons, on Hophni and Phinehas: in one day they shall die, both of them. Then I will raise up for Myself a faithful priest who shall do according to what is in My heart and in My mind. I will build him a sure house, and he shall walk before My anointed forever.

1 Samuel 2:34

We all know, as the account continues, that the ark of God was captured and the glory of the Lord departed! What went wrong? Who had the error?

We think that the sons caused the error, but in reality as we look at the events we can see that **the error**

was in the father. The sons' sin was a result of an error in leadership that allowed an atmosphere of sin before God!

Eli knew that the sin was taking place. He knew that his sons who were the priests were corrupt, but he didn't remove them. The Bible clearly says that he honored his sons more than God (1 Samuel 2:29). This is what I call a spirit or an attitude of error—when people make choices from their hearts or their carnal natures rather than from sound obedience to the principles of God. This action brings judgement from God and creates an opportunity for James 3:16 selfish and carnal leadership that becomes a doorway for every evil thing.

Another example of this is found in 2 Samuel 15 where we read about a son who sat at the gate of the city and undermined his father for forty years!

> **And with Absalom went two hundred men invited from Jerusalem, and they went along innocently and did not know anything. Then Absalom sent for Ahithophel the Gilonite, David's counselor, from his city—from Giloh— while he offered sacrifices. And the conspiracy grew strong, for the people with Absalom continually increased in number.**
>
> **2 Samuel 15:11-12**

Absalom won the hearts of the people and turned them away from their leader. *The conspiracy grew strong!*

We can tell from V:11 that David never talked to or dealt with his son about what he was doing to undermine his leadership. He never let people know his son was out of order! This is a serious mistake Pastors make all the time. We don't want to hurt anyone's feelings or to look like we are against anyone, so we don't let anybody know what is happening when behind the scenes someone is rising up against us. We should let our key leaders know that we are having some concerns and troubles with someone so they are at least aware that something isn't right and will guard themselves so they don't get caught in the conspiracy unaware that anything is wrong!

This was a spirit or attitude of error working in a father towards his son. He made a choice to avoid dealing with it because he loved his son! Just like Eli, it was an error that brought trouble and eventually the sons were lost anyway. It has the same result in a church!

The spirit of error is when a father allows himself to think with his heart instead of remaining faithful and obedient to the word of God. When we rely on our carnal thoughts and feelings in place of the instruction of God we have just functioned in a spirit of error and opened the doorway for the next spirit to work.

This can happen on a corporate level in a community as well! It is seen when leaders made a choice that seemed right in their natural thoughts and feelings instead of waiting on or asking God. Ahab got to be king because the nation chose Omri to defend them instead of seeking God for a leader after His own heart. When I read the story it sounds like a Wild West show that hired a gunfighter to defend them, who later became the corrupt marshal in control of the town. Instead of waiting on the Lord for His choice of a leader, they chose someone who would defend them against their enemies, but later, as the leader, he became the problem himself.

> **But Omri wrought evil in the eyes of the LORD, and did worse than all who were before him.**

1 Kings 16:25

This passed to the next generation and Ahab became even worse.

> **And Ahab the son of Omri did evil in the sight of the LORD above all who were before him.**
> [Even worse than his father Omri]

1 Kings 16:30

Ahab's leadership dynamic allowed Jezebel to partner with him to do her evil work. Jezebel or any other demonic force needs a doorway to come in and the co-operation of people in leadership to function. The actual doorway or error is in creating an environment that allows a James 3:16, carnal, selfish leadership to get established. Leviathan (Jezebel, control, etc.) partners with and takes advantage of this environment.

I. The "spirit of Leviathan"

The first spirit is a ruling force or what I define as a principality. We will all have to deal with it as we rise up into our calling and start to take our cities for Jesus. We face it when we are looking for the redemptive purpose and the violations to that purpose (or what went wrong and got it off track). We tend to go after things the devil has done or the result of the violation.

When we do, we are really only putting a band-aid on the problem. We need to go after the root.

The root of all problems is found in Leviathan. Job 41 says he is the monarch or king over all the children of pride! He rules and reigns with fear and intimidation. He hates the anointing or anybody that functions in the anointing because he is in reality the anti-christ or the anti-anointed one—the one that's against the anointing!

Leviathan is a master of deception and he hides behind the smoke screens of other devils and issues of man to keep his location a secret. To the natural man the devil puts up a false front, appearing to be something good for the city, but behind it all is corruption, greed and power.

II. The spirit of strife

When a father deals with the issues of leadership and headship with his heart instead of with Biblical principles it opens the doorway for strife.

Midian means strife and contention or division, and in Judges 6 we see how this spiritual power works.

> *Then the children of Israel did evil in the sight of the LORD.* [Violation] *So the LORD delivered them into the hand of Midian for seven years,* [Judgement] *and the hand of Midian* [strife and division] *prevailed against Israel. Because of the Midianites, the children of Israel made for themselves the dens, the caves, and the strongholds which are in the mountains.* [Caused God's people to retreat into the caves!]

So it was, whenever Israel had sown, Midianites would come up; also Amalekites and the people of the East would come up against them. Then they would encamp against them and destroy the produce of the earth [destroy their harvest] *as far as Gaza, and leave no sustenance for Israel, neither sheep nor ox nor donkey. For they would come up with their livestock and their tents, <u>coming in as numerous as locusts;</u> both they and their camels were without number; and they would enter the land <u>to destroy it</u>.*

So Israel was <u>greatly impoverished because of the Midianites,</u> [strife and division] *and the children of Israel cried out to the LORD.*

Judges 6:1-6

I looked at the principles here in this passage and identified with verse 6. I said, "Lord, this is our churches today! We are preaching the blessings and prosperity of God, but we live in the reality of lack and poverty."

This isn't just in our finances. Many people I was working with at the time had money but they still had a poverty mentality that kept them bound. So, I backed up to verse 4 and saw that the produce (the intended blessing of God) wasn't actually lost, it had been destroyed!

I saw that the body of Christ today was doing what God's people did in verse 2 by making for ourselves caves to hide in and strongholds (we call churches) to feel safe. I kept backing it up until I saw a great principle in verse 1 that shows that God's people did evil in the sight of the Lord and *He delivered them into*

the hand of the enemy!

This book is based on this principle! We have prayer ministries, deliverance ministries, and churches all over the world that are shouting at the devils of their land. We have whole cities speaking the word of God in corporate prayer crusades and spiritual warfare strategies. The problem is that, for the most part, it hasn't had much measurable fruit to show we really have the power we say we do.

The reason we aren't getting the results we want is that we are busy trying to chase darkness instead of just turning on the lights! So here we see how the Midianite spirit or the spirit that robs your harvest works. When we get close to our harvest of blessings, strife comes in and robs all that we planted and worked so hard to grow. When strife comes don't fight, don't hide and don't get into fear. Stand fast and hold the ground with humility and integrity until you get your harvest into your hands!

We have many churches in our nation that are hurting financially. I believe that they are sowing and watering, but as soon as they are close to reaping a harvest, strife comes and takes it from them!

Don't fight...stand! Get your harvest and then see if there is anything that really is worth fighting against that's still there! I find that most of the time what is left after strife is defeated isn't worth paying much attention to.

This spirit of strife works in the people. It watches for doorways of carnality and uses carnal nature to bring division. It usually is an issue of who can sit at the right or left hand (position). This issue isn't induced by devils, but devils will use our nature as a doorway.

The two camps that are created out of strife and division are like this. One camp usually has the traditions of the house. They say things like, "That's not the way we do things around here!" They are the ones that sit on the boards and have control of the finances. The next generation (not by age but in experience of God) have what I will call a contemporary, new-every-morning experience of God happening in their lives. This two camp environment allows for the next spirit to develop...

III. The spirit of rebellion.

> **For rebellion is <u>as the sin of witchcraft</u>, And stubbornness is as iniquity and idolatry. Because you have rejected the word of the LORD, He also has rejected you from being king."**
>
> **1 Samuel 15:23**

Witchcraft in the house!

When we think of witchcraft we tend to think only of the demonic realms and don't even consider God's people.

I say that the strongest and most powerful form of witchcraft on the earth today is when God's own people use their position, power and influence against the purposes or the people of God! The two camps start to speak against each other and it has power like witchcraft!

The traditionalists look at the contemporaries and reject their experience. The contemporaries look at the traditionalists and say that they are old-fashioned and outdated so they reject and speak against the traditions established in the house. As the two camps speak against one another it has power like witchcraft and it neutralizes the effectiveness of the house of God. The Pastor gets caught in the middle and has no way to win, so he or she can't move the church forward without a battle!

This is a stewardship violation! It can be from a church board or leadership team that had decision-making power and did what seemed right in their own eyes, but went against the purposes, vision or the people of God!

It is full blown when intercessors, key families or influential people of the church use their influence against the pastors or leaders. They may sound right or appear to have the right intentions but they are establishing contradictory words against the vision or the direction the leadership wants to go. It may come out like this..."Lord I know the Pastor means well but..." or, "If I was the leader..."

The Bible says if you declare a thing it will be established for you. We think this refers only to when we are speaking a prophecy or something good. In reality, however, the principle works both ways, for good or evil. When we get together and do the Christian thing we all call "sharing" in a coffee shop or home it has power as we speak words against other people. When we agree together it has even more power. This is witchcraft in the house!

Principalities and powers

This is how I see the spiritual forces working in our nation. The spirit of Leviathan is always trying to influence the minds of natural man to establish a James 3:16 leadership dynamic that it can work through. Leviathan rules over the two other powers of strife and rebellion. Strife is over powers like offence, negativity and division and Rebellion is a strongman spirit over other powers like independence, selfishness or an Absalom-type spirit. I would chart it something like this:

Principality: *Spirit of Leviathan*
Through an "Attitude of error!" - (Doorway)
Brings spiritual powers like:

1. Spirit of Strife: followed by:
    - Offence
    - Negativity
    - Division
2. Spirit of Rebellion: followed by:
    - Witchcraft
    - Independence
    - Selfishness
    - Absalom

Strife and rebellion robs the anointing and perverts authority. We need to repent of witchcraft in the house. When we do it re-activates the anointing to do what the Lord has called us to do. Proper use of the anointing restores the authority and shuts down the strife and division.

How Do We Deal with Leviathan?

Can you fill his skin with harpoons, Or his head with fishing spears? Lay your hand on him; <u>Remember the battle—Never do it again</u>! Indeed, any hope of overcoming him is false; Shall one not be overwhelmed at the sight of him? No one is so fierce that he would dare stir him up.

Job 41:7-10

Our intercessors took it to the Lord and asked, "If we can't fight Leviathan or kill him what do we do?"

The Lord showed them that he feeds off of the dust of the earth!

So the LORD God said to the serpent: "Because you have done this, You are cursed more than all cattle, And more than every beast of the field; On your belly you shall go, And you shall <u>eat dust All the days of your life</u>.

Genesis 3:14

> *And the LORD God <u>formed man of the dust of the ground</u>, and breathed into his nostrils the breath of life; and man became a living being.*
>
> ### Genesis 2:7

Our carnal man is the dust he feeds off! We can't kill him **but we can starve him out** when we refuse to buy into his offences and temptations on our carnal nature! Our leadership teams need to have a loyalty to each other that goes beyond our emotions or our carnal nature's thoughts and feelings, and certainly beyond the circumstances we are facing!

We can all confront it like Jehu did, but ultimately God's plan is a corporate effort to starve it out and build an army that has a heart for God like David did!

Repairing the violation: I've been redeemed!

When we say we have been redeemed by the blood of the Lamb we are saying more than the fact that we are on our way to heaven. God had a plan for our lives from before we were born, and if we could enter a sinless world and make right decisions all the days of our lives we would walk in His plan to the fullest.

The problem is that I made many bad choices and many mistakes that went against what God intended for me to be and for me to do. When I gave my life to Jesus Christ He didn't just forgive me and leave me where I was at, He started to redeem me back into the fullness of His original plan (my redemptive purpose). So now that I have been around for a while,

I believe that the Lord has redeemed me or restored me back into His plan just as though I was never off track in the first place.

It's the same for a city. When we remove the legal rights of the devil to be there and build a new governmental structure to replace him, he has to go! This sets the community free and opens the heavens for the blessings of God. There is then a greater awareness and hunger for God and church. This causes the churches that are lifting up the name of Jesus to prosper and grow!

To correct a violation we go through a process. We are called to a specific city or sphere of influence by geographical boundaries or by people group. If we are where God wants us to be and doing what He has created us to do, we will have all the necessary elements to bring our community back into its redemptive purpose.

Our strengths will move the city forward in vision. But even more importantly, our weaknesses will be a key to identifying the violation.

Our calling to a specific city will put us through the same type of test that people who went before us went through, just as David's test was of the same nature as Saul's. If we respond the same way those that went before us responded, we will have the same results and another generation will pass by until someone else responds to the challenge. If we do what David did and stand faithful to God, relying on and following His instructions even beyond our ability to understand in the natural, we will return in the power of the Spirit and be able to identify the violations and the strongholds. We will also know what to do about it because we had to fight and win it in our own lives first even before we knew what it was.

By the time you can name the spiritual stronghold you are fighting you have already won the battle against it in yourself. **You have personal spiritual supremacy!** Now all you have to do is translate the same principles to the city or region.

We tend to think that in spiritual warfare it works like this: 1) I see it, 2) I fight it, and 3) I win it. But, in actual fact, it's the other way around: 1) I fight it, 2) I win it, and **then 3) I see it!**

The stronghold you are looking for was established because of a violation in the hedge of protection God placed around the redemptive purpose for the city. Sin is judged already so it allows an evil spirit the legal right to be there. It won't go away until we repent before God for the violation. I want to say it again—**we have to determine cause and effect**. We need to find the decisions made in history or the error that looked right to man but shifted the city away from its redemptive purpose! When we repent for these decisions, it removes the devil's right to be there and we are given the spiritual authority to drive it out!

We get the knowledge of the violation the same way David did. He went through the same circumstances as Saul, but he did what Saul **should have done** and his kingdom was established forever!

God won't show you the devils first. He will allow similar circumstances to develop to put you into a place to test your heart and life in the same way as those who failed and committed the violation. I believe there are many people over the years who have been brought to the place of pressure to correct the violations for their city or nation but didn't understand the process and made wrong choices and in so doing, allowed the violation to continue on. Many just give up, many are taken out, and many don't try to Pastor their city so they don't even see the greater significance of the battle they are in.

By the time you can name the spiritual stronghold, you have already got a good understanding of how it works and how to defeat it because you have already won it in your personal life! So the next step is to build a team or the government of God to displace the ruling powers in the heavenlies. This is done by applying the principles that gave you the personal victory to the city.

I asked God to give me the keys of our city, and He did. We should be careful what we are asking for! When we ask God for any anointing or for our city He will answer the prayer by showing you "by experience" what went wrong. If you respond beyond your natural thoughts and feelings and walk by faith, the right choices you make at the point of violation will give you the keys you need to transform your city or even a nation! You win it within yourself first!

When the revelation becomes confirmed by natural knowledge, I want to say to you again, "Don't chase darkness—turn on the lights!" Proclaim the redemptive purpose of the city and build a government to carry it out. It takes a government to replace a government.

There are many types and levels of spiritual government. We have always tried to work through the city ministerial. The problem is that the ministerials of our nation are democratic in nature and most are not structured for a strategic approach to lead our city. The Lord is showing me that the ministerial has a very important part to play in the future well being of any city, but the direction-setting influence is really in the hands of the business sector. I think a city spiritual government made up of Christian leaders from every sector who can develop city-impact strategies would be more able to effect change. They are the successful experts of their areas and have long-term vision and interests in the well being of the community. The church needs to get spiritual supremacy in the city, but the influence or the release of that spiritual authority is from every sector doing its part for the glory of God!

When we get personal spiritual supremacy over the regional spiritual powers, we are elevated in spiritual warfare principles to a higher level or a higher office of spiritual authority.

It's like the person I described earlier who holds a position in a local or municipal government and gets a promotion to provincial government. They find themselves, overnight, in a new position, but they really don't know anything more than they did the day before. The difference is that now the same words they spoke yesterday have more impact today. This isn't because they got wiser over night. It's because in the new office their words carry more power and have more influence. It's the same in the spiritual realm, the higher our spiritual authority, the more impacting our words are, and the more influence God releases to us in the natural realm.

We are dealing with principalities and powers and

rulers of the spiritual realm. They won't go anywhere until we make God happy by going before Him with identificational repentance. By this I mean going before God and asking His forgiveness for the violations we caused to His plans and purposes, (Even if they were done years ago by our forefathers, the influence of the sin is generational. This is when the leaders of a region did what seemed to be right in their own thoughts and feeling but violated the purposes of God.)

When we make it right with God it removes the devils' legal rights to be there. As the lights come on in the city, the devils are exposed and they are creatures of darkness so they have to flee from the light!

Finding the violation

Many ask me, "How do we find the violation?" This is a good question. Here's what we did.

When I got personal spiritual supremacy I could see how the spiritual powers got in because I had to fight it within myself as a weakness. My weaknesses were a match to the violation. I believe that the reason we see some churches breaking into revival for no apparent reason is that they are doing the right kind of ministry that is needed to carry out the redemptive purpose of the city even though they don't know it. I have some thoughts that would lead me to believe that your weaknesses will match and reveal the violations, while your strengths will match and loose the city's redemptive purpose! You have to think about Pastoring your city to even try to understand or see it.

A city with a move of God happening that is focused on repentance probably has a violation that was pride or rebellion. A city that has a move of God happening that is focused on the intimacy of God probably has a violation of rejection or independence. Therefore, the principles can only have effective transition to another region if the violation is relatively the same! If not, they will have either no effect at all or, even worse, a negative effect on our city.

I will give you a brief, basic list to follow:

1. Get personal spiritual supremacy by identifying and dealing with your weaknesses.

2. Know your personal redemptive purpose. Why do you exist? If you are where God wants you to be, your city will be just a larger reflection of your strengths and weaknesses.

3. Build a corporate governmental team—first in your church then in your city. This includes training a skilled intercessory prayer team to work under the governmental leadership team.

4. Do a study on the repetitive cycles in the community. The violation will cause cycles that can be seen in both church and secular history. (What is important to keep in mind is that there is cause and effect. We are looking for root causes in violation corrections, not the effects or results.)

5. Trace history back to a time when the cycles weren't there.

6. Determine when the cycles started and that will give you the timeframe of the violation.

7. Through intercession and natural research determine what went wrong. (Find the error where leaders did what looked to be right in the natural but it allowed a doorway for James 3:16 leaders to rise up with selfish ambition against the purposes of God.)

8. Identify the violation that followed (the sinful acts). The stronghold of a region will match the violator's weaknesses. The error of the fathers or leaders of a region created the doorway, but the violation is the sins that occur as a result of, or after the error. If he or she was weak in greed, God gave them over to their reprobate minds and it was established in the region. If their weakness was pride he would give them over to it, but the judgement would be established as self-centered idolatry, which leads to self idolatry which leads to depression and suicide. Go before God and identify with the violation and ask His forgiveness. (This removes the devil's legal rights to be there.)

9. Do identificational repentance for the error of the leaders and for the violations (sinful acts) that followed.

10. Ask God to reveal the redemptive purpose and to help you to redeem your city into it.

11. Establish vehicles of influence to process the redemptive purpose throughout the community.

Now I want to get to the heart of the reason for writing this book and why I was going to call it...

"The Systematic Sovereignty of God!"

As I have already said, God has many systems that He works sovereignly through. Salvation is one of these.

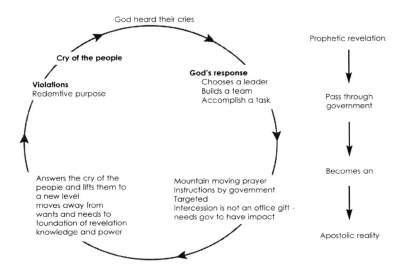

God heard their cries

Cry of the people

Violations
Redemtive purpose

God's response
Chooses a leader
Builds a team
Accomplish a task

Answers the cry of the people and lifts them to a new level moves away from wants and needs to foundation of revelation knowledge and power

Mountain moving prayer
Instructions by government
Targeted
Intercession is not an office gift - needs gov to have impact

Prophetic revelation

Pass through government

Becomes an

Apostolic reality

I made this chart to try and illustrate what I see in total process of the kingdom of God.

We have already covered the issues of redemptive purpose and violations, so I want to draw attention to the result of or the effect of violations to God's principles.

When we find ourselves in the consequences of the violations we are like the people of the Old Testament who were in bondage in Egypt. They cried out to God. I can't tell if they cried out from a heart that was hungry for God or not, but I suspect it had more to do with the conditions they found themselves in. In any case, it seems that tough situations motivate men to start calling upon the name of the Lord. We tend to cry out to God initially from our wants and needs (at least what we think we need). God hears our cries, just like He heard the cries of the people in the days of Moses. What I find significant is what He did to answer the cries of the people. **He rose up a leader!**

The rise of the prayer ministry today has had the same results in the body of Christ. He has heard the cries of the people and now He is rising up leaders around the world to answer that cry. Every organization everywhere is being stirred to train leaders.

Here is where He is Sovereign. Man would choose another Saul—God chose David! God makes the decision of who He rises up to answer the cry of the people. Many times when we see who is responding, they appear to be the last ones we would have chosen. Man looks at the outward appearance, but God deals with the attitudes of the heart! He knows the ones with the right heart attitude who will obey His instructions and do His will in answer to the prayers of the people. Here is where trouble usually comes. The people don't always like the choice God makes and they refuse to follow the leader He sends them.

Authority verses anointing

In the past few years I have noticed another principle at work in the kingdom of God (specifically) and the world at large (generally). There is a tension between authority and the anointing. Many churches have been pulled apart by tension. There are many who have great gifting in the body of Christ but refuse to be a part of a team or refuse to be accountable to anyone but themselves and God Himself. Many gifted preachers, worship leaders, teachers, prophetic people, intercessors or marketplace leaders have trouble with the thought of coming under the covering of a local church or being accountable to the local church pastor. The reason they are reluctant to be under the covering of the Pastor's ministry isn't an issue of rebellion; it's an issue of ability. Many are more gifted in the body than the pastor. The quicker we can come to terms with this truth as pastors, the sooner we can get on with a fruitful ministry. We aren't the most gifted people in the body but we are called to lead and care for those who are!

We have a two-way tension built on the strength of gifting or anointing of the people and the responsibility the pastor is faced with to lead and care for the people, speak into their lives and challenge them in the ways of the Lord. Many look at their pastors as people who couldn't do anything else in life so they went into the ministry. There is a truth to the limited ability part. Most of us as pastors are general practitioners. We are like the family Doctor. We have a broad knowledge of everything but a deep or detailed knowledge of very little. That's why we have medical specialists. This isn't from being lazy, stupid or out of touch, it really is part of being a pastor. In any given day we will deal with someone sick or a family member facing death and the next person celebrating a birth of a baby. We need to be compassionate one minute and celebrative the next. It comes with the calling. Most pastors have the ability to connect to the heart of the people in any situation of life. Where we fall short many times is in management skills, practical application of the knowledge we have, or the lack of success in our personal financial life. It creates an impression, and in some cases it's a reality, that pastors in general have great hearts but lack in wisdom when it comes to the marketplace or even in the specialty ministries of the house of God. Those who have great gifting and anointing then see surrendering their ministry or their abilities to the accountability of a pastor as a step down or a containment of their success. This is due to the gauge we are using to measure the situation.

If my life is measured by my bank account I have limited success and limited potential to release something into your life. But if you measure my life by the calling of God, influence, passion and effectiveness in ministry, leadership ability and experience, determination, team building or any of these gauges, I would have a considerable success factor. The point is this. There are many in my church who are more gifted than I am in worship leading, prayer, leadership training, the marketplace or any other field. There are certainly larger bank accounts than mine and people of greater community influence. My job isn't to control their lives—it's to create environments that increase their knowledge of God, build their character, establish healthy and fruitful relationships and facilitate their success.

We are here for the equipping of the saints for the work of the ministry. That's the purpose in itself. The saints are the ones to actually do the work. We are here to equip and resource them and to walk with them as they become good at being themselves, using all of their gifts, talents, influence and success for the glory of God.

The fact of the matter is this: many are more gifted than I am in the local church, but that doesn't mean that anyone carries a greater responsibility before God than I do. I don't run everything in the church but I am responsible before God for it. If things go wrong the buck stops at my desk. I can't blame the board, the worship leader, the people or even the devil—it's the responsibility that comes with the role of pastor. Pastoring isn't about authority, it's about responsibility, just like in a family the parents have authority over a child's life because they carry the most responsibility. Those who carry the responsibility are given the authority. And just like the family, if you refuse to take the responsibility your authority can be removed. I don't see myself as the one with the greatest gifting or authority. I see it as the one who has the greatest responsibility and as long as we are good stewards, God gives us the authority.

Those who are charged with the responsibility are given the authority; it isn't about who is the most gifted. We tend to give the people in the church broad responsibility but limited direction-setting authority. We keep the decision making to the board or pastoral team. In the area of accountability, vision or general care of the people this is ok, but in terms of gifting and abilities it can be a limiting factor to the growth and strength of the church in itself. If we control or mandate gifting by programs and rules we are actually limiting the success of those who may have the ability to rise higher than the guidelines we have set. In this case the pastor or the program becomes a bottleneck or restricting factor in church success. We don't do it intentionally; we are really trying to be responsible, organized and protective of the well being of the people God has given us to care for. I understand there are times when pastors have to take a stand or deal with some people or circumstances that are just simply out of order and harmful to the people involved and destructive to the body, these aren't the times I am referring to.

We have to value both authority and anointing. In order to succeed we need both. Overemphasis of either one will bring division and strife every time. Overemphasis of authority will feed a legalistic controlling environment that a religious spirit, or the many other names we could give it, can thrive. An under emphasis of authority allows for a Jezebel-type spirit to move in and cause harm. Overemphasis of giftings without the accountability of authority can allow gifts to lead people by emotion, hype, manipulation, charisma or many other forms. In this environment we have prophecies that don't get judged, teaching that bends the foundational doctrines and reads right off the pages of the reasonable interpretation of the Word. Or we end up with self-serving, self-centered ministries that rise up and lead people away from the corporate church and into a private controlled spiritual club that history has shown can end in disasters and death.

There is a place for authority in the house if it's a healthy authority. There's a place for anointing if it has the right spirit driving it. When we partner the two together in a healthy environment it releases and builds rather than controlling and tearing down. We can learn a great deal about authority and anointing and how they function in the body from the accounts given by those who have gone before us.

Think of Saul and David for a moment. King Saul was chosen by the people and blessed by God to be the one in authority. He was also anointed or given the gifting and favor of God to be the king. So he had both authority and anointing working in his life. This continued until he violated the instructions of God and performed the sacrifice and caused the violation I spoke of earlier. When he disobeyed and caused the violation by doing a priestly duty a king was not allowed to do, his destiny and the anointing shifted over to a man after God's own heart, the little shepherd boy, David. Now Saul had the authority but David had the anointing.

We can learn a great deal by studying how David used the anointing while honoring authority. We have many stories in the body of Christ where the anointed worship leaders, business leaders or other anointed and gifted people tried to become the pastor by leading a rebellion to overthrow those in power. What generally happens is we lose both authority and anointing in the process. In the attempt to defend ourselves we speak words against the other. These words are doorways of power for the devils. Words from those in authority against the anointing works like witchcraft and contains or limits the flow of the Spirit of God. Words from the anointing against those in authority neutralizes the power of God and the church is contained. God also judges both entities. Notice that when Saul disobeyed the instructions of the Lord he lost the anointing first but still had the authority. God won't release His anointing or His supernatural power on an authority that is out of order with His will or His ways. Receiving the anointing was a heart issue for David. So I believe losing the anointing is also an issue of the heart.

David was anointed to be the king, but Saul was still the one in authority. David was very careful not to touch Saul. He knew God had blessed him to be the king and it was up to God to deal with Saul. David used his gifts to lead the people rather than challenge the king. We can measure the degree of his commitment. A church will reflect the teaching, the character and the attitudes of those who equipped them. When Saul died all of David's men mourned the death of Saul. They all had the same heart to honor those whom God had placed in leadership. He was loyal beyond the faults of the king.

The Bible teaches us that we reap what we sow, and David's harvest was faithful men of valor around him. The principle here is this. If you want loyalty sow seeds of loyalty, if you want commitment plant the seeds in your own life, and so on with passion, accountability, etc. (many pastors want people to come under their authority when they themselves don't have true accountability working in their lives).

God took care of Saul. He gave Saul time to repent, instructions to change and opportunity to continue to lead the nation. But without the anointing or the favor of God on his life he continued to struggle, fall short and fail. We see this all the time in ministries who have violated a principle of the Lord. We see very gifted people who have a chip on their shoulder about authority. This limits the release of the anointing and can even be a doorway for devils (James 3:16 principle). When this happens we have ministries that look right, sound impressive, do all the right things but release a wrong spirit into the church. In the days we live in there are incredibly talented people in the body of Christ. Now, more than ever, we need discernment to know the spirit working through these gifts and abilities.

The Spirit of the Lord left Saul and came on David. A distressing spirit of the Lord came on Saul. He became paranoid and confused and made all kinds of excuses. He even blamed the people. We see this happen all the time in the church world. Pastors abuse their authority or refuse to walk in obedience to what the Lord wants done and the anointing leaves them.

Confusion, depression and blame-shifting settle in. This is a critical time in the house of God. If the ones who have the anointing rise up against the ones in authority to overthrow those in power the anointing of God is removed from them as well. Now we have a dysfunctional authority and gifts that are man-driven rather than anointed or moved by God.

This is a healthy environment for devils and the carnal nature, but the Spirit of God is contained until we repent or turn around the other way. At all costs we need to protect our anointing by our attitudes, actions and words. This doesn't mean we can't speak out or address issues with those in authority. It's not a question of "if" we can do it, it's more in the area of "how" we do it that makes the difference. If we speak out and stir up strife in the body we create an environment where the authority is neutralized and the anointing is lost.

This is one of the main reasons I will only come under the authority of those who are under authority. You have authority when you are under authority. I'm not the one to correct those who rule over me in the Lord. I can raise issues and concerns, I can speak my mind and I can challenge ideas with better ideas, but I must do it in an honoring way. If I honor those who rule over me in the Lord, I can maintain the anointing God has placed on my life even if the ideas I put forward are rejected and not used. If what I felt led to do was of God, He is able to deal with those in authority.

If I start to undermine or speak against those God has put in authority, I am coming into agreement with devils and they will tap into my gifting and influence and witchcraft will be loosed in the house of the Lord. The highest form of witchcraft is when God's own people use their position and power against God's purpose or His people. Witchcraft has no authority on its own. All authority was given to the Son and He gave it to His church. Devils watch for this kind of environment. They start to tap into the defensive words of those in authority and those who are anointed. This gets the two camps fighting and focuses both strengths inward. The situation starts to look like a firing squad standing in a circle shooting at each other.

David knew enough to leave Saul's destiny to God. He controlled what he was responsible for: his words, attitudes and deeds. When Saul's chances came to an end, God took care of it. It was in the Lord's hands to determine when enough was enough. But when He did, the authority that was on Saul's life shifted over to the one who had been faithful with the anointing.

There is much to learn here. When we are looking for the violations and trying to restore our cities we need to trace the cycles of both the authority and anointing. Who had the authority? How did they use or abuse it? When did it become about man's plan instead of God's? Were there those who rose up against the authority in the wrong way and lost the anointing or the supernatural strength of God? You can find it in cycles. We have found that when the anointing has been removed the work may continue, but it becomes a work of man in his own strength. Trying to do the work of the Lord in our own strength burns us out, defeats us and brings us to discouragement and depression. Most of the time we focus on trying to restore the authority, but in actual fact we need to restore the anointing first. The anointing then strengthens us to fulfill our redemptive purpose, and as we walk in humility and obedience to fulfill our purpose, God releases more authority!

Jesus went into the wilderness in Luke 4 and returned in the power! This power strengthened Him to walk in humility, meekness and favor with God and man on His journey to the cross! Going to the cross fulfilled His purpose and all authority was given unto the Son. This is a repetitive pattern. All authority of God is gained through acts of humility and obedience. Every anointing is gained and maintained by having the right attitudes and actions in the face of challenges.

We need to find out where the anointing for our city was lost by an unrighteous act against those in authority. Then we need to go before the Lord and repent of the words and deeds of unrighteousness. This restores the anointing. It restores the supernatural strength we need to do the work of the Lord. Under this strength of God we can walk through to personal spiritual supremacy and "then" we can deal with the violations of those who where in authority before us.

Through this process the violations are corrected, the anointing reactivated and the redemptive purpose of our city is revealed. This allows the authority to be restored, which increases the abilities of God even more.

Here's an example of how it works in the local church. A pastor feels called and responds to a city. He or she gives their lives to leading the people God has given them. However, if they are in the right place their strengths may not be the main key to their kingdom. Remember the teaching earlier on how my weaknesses have made me strong. The keys to the city are obtained by getting to a place of personal spiritual supremacy or overcoming your weaknesses. This means the gifts and abilities of the worship leader who wants to overthrow the pastor may be impressive and needed to build the church, but not necessarily the right keys for the kingdom. The irony is that a stronger gifting and charismatic personality could win the battle, but would also be the key factor in losing the war. Those who have authority need to walk in it.

And those who have gifting need to recognize the difference between authority or responsibility and anointing. They are both needed. A pastor with a good heart may not carry the responsibility or use the authority because he doesn't want to offend or hurt anybody's feelings.

This is what happened to David with Absalom. He loved his son so he let him stand at the gate for years undermining his father's leadership.

A pastor can also use authority on the other end of the spectrum. He or she can see the coup rising up in the church and use authority to defend himself or herself against the people. This, too, will stop God's purposes from coming to pass and will open the door for a religious spirit to establish itself in the church. A worship leader may overthrow the pastor due to the great influence and favor they have with the people. This may give more freedom in worship and a more charismatic environment, but it won't transform a city. The devil will defeat you if he can, but if all he does is neutralize your effectiveness and contain your anointing he has still won. We need to have an environment of humble, servant-oriented leadership at every level. Leadership is leadership. We can lead people into the blessings of God and His heart and nature as David did or we can lead people into offence, division and the nature of the devils we were saved from to fight. We all need to be on the same page, heading the same direction, honoring one another in our responsibilities and our gifting.

We can see the pattern in king Saul. He was a leader who followed his own thoughts and feelings instead of obeying the Lord. Confusion sets in, anxiety rises, the leaders get paranoid towards their own people, they seek wisdom from places that doesn't bring God's wisdom and they try to kill those who carry the anointing. From the other side we see leaders who are called to be a part of the team wanting to be the pastor. They manipulate, undermine and generally refuse to co-operate with the direction or instructions of leaders over them. These people will eventually part company. Either the pastor is undermined to a point of lack of confidence in the people in general, or they rise up to defend themselves and the fight is on, sides are chosen, battle lines are drawn and the purposes of God grind to a halt.

Another outcome of this scenario is that the worship leader leaves the church. However, most gifted people have influence with other people, so they rarely leave alone. It can start a landslide of people leaving to follow the gifting because it's what they can see and experience. Authority is not a tangible or experiential entity, it's a principle. We have authority when we are under authority. Many in the body of Christ lack authority because they refuse to be under authority or allow anyone to hold them accountable.

It's not seen in their attendance or lack of it, it's an

issue of the heart. But eventually out of the heart the mouth speaks and it turns to witchcraft. Those who fall into this principle or way, have gifts and influence but never seem to have much positive impact on society in general. This is due to the fact that we need to use authority in the heavenlies over all the powers of the enemy. This breaks the strongholds and opens the heavens for the anointing to flow freely without the obstacles. The gifts and anointing are needed to let natural man tap into the authority of God under an open heaven and deliver the words, ways and presence of God to the people.

The government of God is listed in Ephesians as the apostle, prophet, evangelist and teacher, but more importantly, the function they have is stated as well, "for the equipping of the saints for the work of the ministry!" The authority has the responsibility to equip the saints but it's the saints with all of their gifts and abilities that actually do the work of the ministry. In the North American church we have this backwards. We tend to want the anointed or gifted ones to have the say, tell us what direction to go and how to get there and then tell the pastors what they should be doing. Any pastor that allows this environment to be established in the local church is heading for burnout.

We, as pastors, need to love the people, but we also need to take responsibility for the direction the Lord wants the church to go. We need to stand strong in establishing the vision, direction and well being of the church, but at the same time we need to allow the gifted ones to get us there! Those who are gifted need to honor the office God has put in place and trust He will deal with the leaders if they don't go the direction He wants them to go. I understand there are times when the issue isn't authority or anointing but a clash of personalities. That's a whole different problem.

Gifted people who speak against those who carry the responsibility will eventually lose the anointing or God's help with their gifts. Leaders who abuse their authority or don't take the responsibility to lead the people where the Lord wants them to go will lose the mantle of authority just like king Saul did. We need both authority and anointing working in harmony in the local church to defeat the devil, free the people and take the land. Abuse of one neutralizes the other.

The leaders have a special task ahead of them. They will be expected to lead the way, as always, but now there is an awareness of an even greater responsibility to God and man. This is to move the body of Christ from "Prophetic Revelation" to an "Apostolic Reality!"

We have all heard the words that have come from conferences and churches for many years now. Every church, every organization and every nation has words that witness to us about our purpose as individuals and as a body for the direction and call of God. These revelations have to be brought into some kind of order to make sense. All revelations need to be judged and put into some sort of order and strategy to become a reality. Are they past, present of future? Personal, church or city? This is what leaders are called to do. They will be given the gifting, ability and inspiration they need to build a team to accomplish the task that God has given to them.

The revelations that are coming from the prayer

meetings all seem to have significance to the big picture, but someone has to determine how they fit and what strategy is to be used as well as what the timing is to implement them. This takes the leadership of the Pastor with a governmental team.

I would like to make a small side note here. In the intercessory prayer meetings I have attended in the last five years I have made some observations. One is that they are predominantly attended by women. I have heard it said by Cindy Jacobs that "not all intercessors become Prophets, but all Prophets are intercessors." If the ratio of intercessors is predominantly women, I think we can put it together and make an assumption, if not a discernment, *that the probability is that we will hear a strong prophetic voice from the women Prophets in the near future.*

Another observation is that many of the recognized Apostles of our land don't attend the intercessory meetings. This lack of partnering between the present day apostolic movement and the intercessor leaves a gap in what I believe is God's plan of teamwork. Intercession is a gift that some people definitely are stronger in than others. But the statement I would like to make is that **intercession is a gift but it isn't an office ministry!** It doesn't have spiritual governmental authority alone. It is a gift that has authority because it is under authority.

You can make a police uniform and still not have any authority in the land. The authority comes from being under authority! Every Pastor needs to have a Pastor—not just in name or administrative principle but an actual working relationship. Every intercessor that tries to challenge the powers of the enemy has the same need.

We all need to have someone to watch over us that we trust beyond our personal revelations. We need this so that if we are getting off track or heading in a direction that we can get hurt or hurt someone else, there is someone there who will speak into our lives and set us straight. We also need someone to bring encouragement and strength when it is needed. If we don't have people watching over our lives and holding us and our ministries accountable we are an open target for the enemy to little by little lead us astray, and the ultimate end of this behavior is hurting a lot of people.

The partnering between Apostles and intercessors results in targeted prayers with governmental power bringing "Prophetic Revelation to an Apostolic Reality!"

Review of how to build your governmental team.

1. Determine what God is saying and what He is calling you to do.

2. Break the vision down into categories or defined tasks.

3. Find and start to train a leader to accomplish the defined task who is better at it than you are, i.e. a prayer Pastor, worship leader, youth Pastor, home group leader or any other defined department or task. (Many Pastors feel insecure raising up leaders around them that are better

at a specific task than they are but it has to happen to build a strong team. When the team is built it has to be stronger than the leader can be alone or it isn't going to have any impact.)

When the task has been defined and the leader chosen,

4. Start to build a team around that leader. The team relates to the leader and the leader relates to you or a designated manager of team leaders. The process causes multiplication in the body. When I spend time with one leader who has a team of four people ministering to four or five people each, there has just been personal ministry involvement with 25 or 30 people. So, with ten leaders using this principle, I can minister to 250-300 people with the same amount of my time.

5. The team leader identifies the tasks and builds the team. Then we start to work on strategies with time-based goals. Without setting a time target we tend to never get started. The leader sets the vision or long-term goal or target and then works with the team to identify the reality of where they are starting from, their strengths and weaknesses as a team, and what priorities need to be established.

The team then takes ownership of the process. I have watched teams I have built over the years do things the hard way. They can wander off track at times or get so stuck so they aren't going forward at all. We have to allow the team the decision-making power in the process. Our job as leaders is to watch and see that they will still get to the desired goal even if it is not doing it the way we would with our experience.

We tend to step in too soon and point out the easy way and lay it all out for the team. This seems to be the right thing because it moves them forward. In reality, however, it doesn't build their teamwork in problem solving. They become dependent on your leadership and instructions and become obedient workers but not good problem solvers.

When the leader is trained, the team is built and the tasks are defined.

6. Then we start to look at the prophetic revelations and see how they can all fit into one picture. Each team has a piece of the revelation already defined in their tasks. The challenge for the apostolic leader is to now make each department leader and their team with their defined task work like a football team to strategically and systematically defeat the enemy and push for the common goal line.

7. When the revelations are brought into order and the timing is determined, then the instructions can be sent to the intercessors, including the vision, strategy and strongholds of the enemy against the purposes of God.

This allows prayer with governmental power. The intercessors can now declare a thing and it *will be* established for them.

As I said earlier, we tend to have shotgun blast

prayers into the darkness and we even get lucky enough to hit something once in a while. But I am talking about targeted prayer with the full force of the corporate church behind it, just like the police officer has in the natural. We can then have a whole network of prayer teams praying for a specific city, at a specific time with defined strategies and goals as well as being able to name the strongholds that need to be broken.

In the local church, a city or even a nation this brings an answer back to the cry of the people with an apostolic or governmental reality to it.

I believe this process will return the signs and wonders of the Apostles to the body of Christ. We will move from wants and needs to **a new platform of declaration and commands!**

If you want healing in your church, cry out to God out of that need and He will rise up someone with an ability to lead the way and build a team to accomplish the task. This will answer the cry of the people and release an accountable and effective body ministry to the church. I believe every anointing can be released and every need met by this process!

Apostolic Relationship Communication Network

About seven years ago we developed a system called "Prayer in Action!" We combined it with another system we called the "ARC" Network. This is the "Apostolic, Relationship, Communication, Network!"

The ARC Network

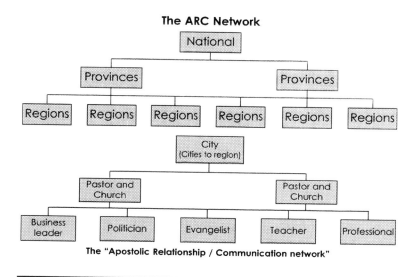

The "Apostolic Relationship / Communication network"

The chart shows the flow of information from an individual to the national network.

The information networks out there now can overload any team. There are so many prayer requests, reports and stories that you can't even begin to keep up with them all. I got to a place where I had to change my E-mail address because every time I opened it I had so many messages I couldn't possibly get any work done. So we developed a communication system to overcome the information overload.

Each person in a church should know their reason to exist or their redemptive purpose. The Pastor should be aware of what each person's redemptive purpose is, so he can help to bring it to a reality as well as knowing the built-in resources and giftings available in the church when they are needed. They can all feed the information for their sector of society to the Pastor and leadership team of the local church for discernment and strategy.

It's the same with the corporate church. We need to know the redemptive purpose or the reason the church exists so we can run with it. Then each church in a city can proclaim their purpose and the strongholds that are holding them back. The city redemptive purpose gives all the churches a common target so the city moves forward in the same direction.

We can document or chart the redemptive purpose for each church, the revelations they have about their city, and the strongholds they are up against. This will give a clearer picture of the state of the spirit realm in that city.

The strategies can be determined by the Pastors and leaders in the city and the tasks defined. This information about the redemptive purpose (of each church, and the cities in the region), the strongholds against it and the citywide strategies to overcome them gets passed to a regional facilitator. They will record all the information for each city in their region.

This combined information will give a clearer picture of the redemptive purpose and the strongholds of each region. The information is then sent to a provincial facilitator who records the information for all the regions outlined in his or her province. The provincial purpose, as well as the strongholds against it, will then be easier to define and confirm by natural knowledge (spiritual mapping) as we will be able to see (like building a puzzle) what God is doing in each region. This provincial information will be given to the national network so they can pray with full knowledge of the redemptive purpose, strongholds and strategies for any part of our country.

As the Apostolic fathers and leaders review the revelations, redemptive purposes and strongholds in the nation they will then have the information needed to see the big picture and develop national strategies. This will include targeting key strongholds of the enemy, determining which ones need to be addressed first and the planning the timing for strategic events.

When the target is established and the strongholds are identified we can issue prayer instructions to all the teams in the land. These instructions will have the time and place of events or crusades, the purpose for the event and the goals we hope to accomplish. This will allow each Apostolic leader, intercessor and local church to join forces with their prayer power as well as using their influence in that city to promote unity and participation in the event.

The Apostles need the intercessors, but the intercessors also need the governmental authority of the Apostles behind them. If we will work as one, I believe we will see city after city transformed by the gospel of Jesus Christ.

This gives us an Apostolic-Relationship-Communication network!

Our intercessors call this "Prayer in action"

Processing targeted prayer with governmental power works like this:

- Corporate team in local church - teamwork (gathering the pieces of revelation together).

- Revelations given to church government - to bring order and discernment.

- Then the information gets passed on to the city government or relationship Pastors and leaders of the city for discernment and strategy.

- As each church contributes their piece of the revelation God has given the bigger purposes of God for the city can be seen and citywide strategies developed.

- Then the information of Redemptive Purpose, strongholds, and strategies is sent to a regional facilitator.

- The regional strategy information then gets processed to the national prayer center.

Through the prayer centre the information gets distributed to the Apostolic leaders and their prayer teams of the nation to have their governmental proclamations and commands added to ours. The prayer then changes from Prophetic revelation to an Apostolic prayer or an Apostolic reality (Job 22 - Declare a thing...and it will be established for you). But they are not praying shotgun prayers into the dark hoping they will hit something. They will have the information to pray targeted, strategic, governmental prayers of agreement. This has the power to effect change in the heavenlies that will be seen in the natural.

This gives us a prayer network that has targeted prayer with governmental power!

Roles in the
Coming Revival

Roles of the church, marketplace and intercession in city and national transformation.

Church

I have already talked about the "boot camp" principle of the local church being a place where the Lord creates a mock war with all of the noise and actions of the real one He is sending you into. It is a place where we can be equipped, gain experience and develop a strength of soul for the real enemy and the real war out in the marketplace.

There is another principle I would like to address regarding the local church and its role in transformation:

The "Path of the Least Resistance!"

In the recent months I have heard many teachings about the coming wave of God to our cities and nations. The teaching claims that the next move of God will begin in the marketplace and not the local church. The premise is given that in the majority of accounts in the New Testament the miracles happened in the marketplace rather than in the local church. When I heard this teaching I had some reservations, so I started to think about what this was saying. It would mean that we, as local church pastors, would then just wait until the wave of God swept through our city and eventually made it to the church. I may be prideful, but this thought bothered me. I had no intention of sitting and waiting for someone else to do what I had committed to doing when I entered the clergy ministry. So I started to seek the Lord and ask Him to teach me. The revelation came in a very strange but clear and powerful way.

My wife Kim and I were attending a conference in Honolulu, Hawaii, and took an afternoon to drive to the north shore to see the winter season's thirty-five foot waves. This in itself is an experience, but there turned out to be a greater purpose for us being there. I watched the powerful waves rising out of the horizon with ever increasing size and strength as they came near the shore. As amazing as the waves were, I was even more amazed at the surfers who rushed out to catch the biggest ones they could find and ride them. Some had great success, while others had spills that caused my body to wince with pain as I watched the pounding waves burry them under millions of gallons of water with the force of an out-of-control freight train.

As I watched I started to see patterns in the waves. Some would break left, others right, and some would crash into each other causing a spiral of water to shoot into the air. I started to ponder what caused these waves to respond in such an out-of-control yet almost predictable repetitious behavior.

There is a surfer we have spent some time with during our last couple of visits to the island. He paints in the morning, then heads to the north shore for the afternoon to catch the big waves. I asked him how the waves were formed. He informed me that they were formed by the wind. I instantly got an unction of the Holy Spirit that there was a spiritual parallel that I was to pay attention to. The waves have no will of their own and no power to determine their own destiny, so what determined the direction they took as they approached the shore? The thought came to me that it was the shape of the landscape that determined the flow. The waves follow the contour of the land.

Through this observation the Lord taught me about the coming wave of His presence. The wave is generated by the wind of the Spirit. You can see it coming in the horizon in many cities and even nations today.

The body of Christ has had a surfer mentality throughout the years. We grab our spiritual ministries and gifts like surfboards and swim out into the deep waters to catch the waves! We ride the raw energy of God with skill and finesse, cheering each other on and applauding the new moves or courageous maneuvers. As each wave passes we swim back out into open waters and bob up and down until the next wave comes.

The Lord spoke to me and said that He didn't call us

to ride the waves as they came, He called us to shape the landscape to determine the direction the waves will take. What a thought! Our time shouldn't be spent riding the wave but preparing for it! From many years ago in high school I seem to remember a basic law of physics. This law says that water will follow the path of the least resistance. With this thought in mind it was an easy step to see what the Lord was trying to impress upon me. Our job is to make the local church the path of the least resistance for the coming waves of God!

I went back to see if this thought would hold out in scripture. In almost every, if not all, cases recorded in the Bible where there was a move of God that rose up in the marketplace, there was a previous attempt to start it in the local church (which at that time was called a synagogue). In almost every, if not all accounts, the early apostles and even Jesus Himself went first to the local church, but the church was so high and mighty on itself that it wasn't the path of the least resistance, so the raw energy of the wave kept on going past them and into the marketplace with signs and wonders and miracles. This would have happened in and though the local church if it would have been prepared to receive it.

I started to think about church history and saw a similar pattern. Organizations throughout church history have caught a wave of truth and have ridden it for years even though, for the most part, the energy and power has passed. Human nature throughout history has proven that we will hang on to a past truth even to the elimination of a present reality. When a new wave of God arrives, the churches that were built on the last wave are not ready or open to receiving anything that doesn't fit the past experiences so they resist the new to preserve the familiar.

The raw wave of God knows no boundaries, respects no person and is limited only by reception or resistance rather than by skill, knowledge, religious ways or hard work. It just comes to anyone who will receive it. When the existing churches are too high and not open to the coming of God, the raw power continues on until it reaches those who will receive it.

In the accounts of the Bible we see the wave or the coming presence of God attempt to come to and through the local church, but being resisted there, it continued on out into the marketplace to those who would receive. This has re-occurred many times in church history. The wave is rejected and so passes by established churches and organizations and flows out to the marketplace where a whole new church or denomination gets birthed.

We need to work hard at becoming the path of the least resistance. This doesn't mean we don't have any guidelines or any rules of order. It's actually quite the opposite. We need to get our house in order, programs in place, teams built, vision established and workers entrenched to handle the impact of the coming of the Lord. This kind of thinking blows simply program-based church strategy out of the water. We tend to build a program, find someone to run it and then ask God to fill it. Instead of determining what the Lord is doing, embrace the flow of it and build a program around what He is doing rather than what we want done. When we embrace what the Lord is doing someone usually gets stirred to lead it.

When a leader is stirred by the Lord and not by submission or need they are self-motivated and strong.

So the question remains, Can you actually harness or even hope to prepare for a full-on, raw, direct hit of a giant wave of God? The answer to the question is Yes we can, and we are.

This lesson on the shores of Hawaii was so impacting on my life and ministry that we instantly started to implement programs, philosophies, training and partnerships to create an environment that embraces the waves of God. We have succeeded! Our local church has become the floodgate. We don't control the move of the Spirit but we do harness it!

The main thought remains that we have to shift our mindset from building a church to pastoring our city and then the church will grow as a byproduct.

To do this the local church needs to become the path of the least resistance to the coming presence of the Lord. We need environments for the equipping of the saints for the work of the ministry. This means ministries of all kinds. We tend to focus on worship, prophecy, preaching and other "behind the walls of church" types of ministries. In actual fact, we are to equip the saints for life in and beyond the walls of church. Being good at life or being good at being themselves is their ministry! We say, "We are here to help you be good at being you!"

Character, integrity, work ethics, leadership abilities and marketplace success are all ministry issues we need to build on. Who is training the teachers, the police force, the judges, the politicians, the successful people at large? Most of the time it isn't the local church doing it. We tend to think we can't equip them because we don't have a law degree or haven't done anything outside of being a pastor. This may be true, but the local church can still be the facility of training, mentoring and support for those who do. We don't have to be the experts at everything—we just need to be able to recognize and embrace those who are, and create environments of relationship where they can reproduce themselves in others. We also have a responsibility to equip the saints for life.

Success training isn't just about who gets to lead worship, preach or pastor. These are needed gifts in the house, but the work of the ministry goes way beyond the four walls of the house of the Lord. Our job is to equip people in every way so they can be good at being themselves and by being good at being themselves they become living epistles the world can read and great ambassadors for the Lord.

My goal is to take the gifting or natural tendencies people have and turn them into ministries beyond the walls of church. How does someone naturally gifted or inclined to the prophetic minister in a coffee shop or any other public place in a way an unchurched person would receive and without drawing unusual attention to themselves? How does someone who has a teaching gift use their gift to win souls? How does a worship leader use his or her gift in the secular world? How does someone who is called to be a pastor actually pastor his city beyond the walls or programs of church?

Many great churches are being built around the

world with this kind of strategy: equip the saints to walk in skill and integrity in the marketplace. I am in agreement with this as being a good strategy and the way to pastor our cities. What I add to the thinking is the issue of sustainability. I believe we need to change the spiritual climate of our cities in order to sustain a move of God.

I don't want just our church to grow, I want to see the whole body of Christ break out in explosive growth. I don't expect that just the Christians will be blessed in our city. God causes the rain to fall on all men. We tend to think being blessed by the Lord is an issue of holiness in itself. We think if we are holy we get blessed. This thought has led many to a pursuit of spiritual perfectionism. The Pharisees were on that track and even God wouldn't go to their church. It leads to spiritual blindness, judgmental leadership and a religious program without the presence. Even secular people who are doing what the Lord wants done in a city will be blessed.

There are city ministries that are common, like food and clothing distribution centres. These are needed and must be done, but I believe we can all experience greater blessings of the Lord by aligning ourselves and serving His plan for our city or the reason He created the city in the first place. I call this the Redemptive Purpose and those who recognize it and serve it will find a greater favor with God and man. We didn't get influence in our city by a strategy of infiltration, we got influence by invitation. The greatest measurement of the authority God has given a pastor is the favor on his life or ministry.

Favor in the church but not in the community

defines the sphere of authority and influence God has given him. (Favor in the city but not in the province, favor in the province or nation but not internationally, etc.) Authority can also be measured by favor among people groups. Some have great favor with certain ethnic groups no matter where they find them. Someone may have knowledge about the first nations people but no favor. On the other hand, you could have very little knowledge of their culture or history but have great favor with them. The favor will give you a greater influence than the knowledge in itself.

Favor is a sign of the blessing and presence of God. If it isn't evident it doesn't necessarily mean God isn't with you. But it may mean we are trying to go a direction or influence a sphere or do something He hasn't called us to. To me this is what I call church! Determine and develop your sphere of influence! The four walls of the building or the structured church in itself is the "boot camp" or "training center" to embrace your gift and calling and help you to be good at being you! We are here to facilitate your success.

How do we facilitate success for someone who is already more successful in life than the pastor? I struggled with this for a season of time. I was on the golf course one day and was put with two other men to play a round. These two men were both at least a foot taller than me, both played excellent golf, both were upper managers for major corporations, both had the manners and ways of high level executives...and then there was me.

At that time our church was still small. My finances

were limited. My social experience was blue collar for the most part, and I was new to the game of golf so I was hitting about three shots to their one. This was a grueling but great experience for me. It showed me that I felt intimidated by those above my level of success. Then I realized there was a common principle here for most pastors. We all feel more comfortable pastoring or speaking into the lives of those who are less fortunate, more needy or at a lower social status than we are. For some it's the reason they head for the inner city. It's not as much of a call as a confidence issue. When this kind of ministry gains confidence it starts to shift to another social class.

I was stuck in a trap in my own mind. I was intimidated by those who had greater social status or success than I had. What was I going to do? I couldn't influence the influencers of my city if I was insecure or intimidated so much that my confidence wasn't there. We all know how dumb we can get when we are nervous or lack confidence in something. I needed to come up another level if I wanted to pastor my city. I turned to the Lord and He, as always, gave me a strategy. He told me to do something that would remind me every day of my goal to rise up to another level.

All my life I wore cowboy boots or biker boots. I still like them, but the boots represented an attitude and an image to me. So the Lord told me to get rid of the cowboy or biker boots and get a pair of dress shoes.

This may not seem like a big deal to you, but to me it was a huge public image shift. My boots gave me confidence. They made we walk in what my perception was of a man—strong, tough and ready for a rugged life. When I put on the dress shoes it changed everything. I bought some that had tassels on top of them. I called them my "fairy boots" and they made me feel more like Tinkerbell than a biker. This was hard on the macho image I had of myself and this in itself was the point the Lord was trying to make. If I wanted to rise up to another level it started by the way I saw myself; just like in Joshua's day, if I saw myself like a grasshopper they would too.

There we saw the giants (the descendants of Anak came from the giants); and we were like grasshoppers in our own sight, and so we were in their sight.

Numbers 13:33

How we see ourselves is the root of most issues of success and achievement. An overestimation of skill or ability will get you into trouble, but an underestimation of potential will limit you just the same. I bought the shoes. Now every day, all day, as soon as I put my shoes on in the morning and with every step I take through the day, I have a constant reminder to change!

Now, many years later, I have the privilege of working with and influencing many strong leaders and people of great success. I can now minister to this realm as easily as to those who have great needs.

Everyone has needs. Our job is to walk with them and watch for what my friend Pastor Ed Delph from Phoenix Arizona would say...find what is lacking, wanting or in need of building up. To see what is needed in their lives doesn't take a prophetic gift, it only takes a keen sense of the obvious. The hard part is having the confidence to step into the opportunity and bring the wisdom of God. When I have opportunity to step up into a higher-level ministry, one look down at my "fairy boots" and I'm ready! It reminds me that this was my goal in the first place and inspires me to step forward.

Facilitating success doesn't mean you are the one with the greatest success in the room. It means you are the one who created the environment, gathered the people and determined some flow of the meeting or an agenda. Our job is to recognize those who have gifts and success and create an environment for them to teach, train or impart their success to others. I don't have to be a lawyer to host a meeting for lawyers, etc. My job is recognizing those who have something to offer and then to market and promote the meeting, inviting those who are interested in learning and growing in that field and put them together in a professional environment of excellence. Through this we can facilitate their success.

We can also learn enough of what they need to resource them with the latest materials and books on personal development in their field. We need to learn what they are looking for, who they consider worth listening to or reading about, and what their key personal development goals are and put some work into finding these resources for them.

I buy books for my business owner's group or "professionals" and I give them as gifts. They have all had many pastors come with their hands out wanting but not many have come with their hands out ready to give them what they need. Through this I have developed some new skills, learned to see from their perspective and have risen to a higher level of success and blessing in my own life in the process.

The local church is the greatest place to facilitate success. We tend to avoid talking about success or dealing with wealth. Many would criticize putting effort into this area. The fact is, we can't lead our cities without those of wealth and power and influence. We need to have them on board if we want to really bring transformation. One business person of success and influence can do more for the needy than many churches in our fundraisers and work projects by ourselves. We often have the manpower but don't have the wealth it takes to do something right, so we just work with the volunteers and do the best we can. I'm not suggesting we should stop doing anything we are doing. I am suggesting, however, that we need to find a place for those of wealth and power if we really want to have an impact on our city. One successful business leader can gather a crowd, sell the vision and raise more money for the needy in one night than a pastor could do in offerings and fundraisers in a year.

Learn to walk with them. There are reasons they are successful and it's not just that they got the breaks, many of them created the breaks. They were in the right place at the right time but not by accident, it was by discipline, preparedness and awareness of opportunity. They develop their abilities and increase their knowledge so when opportunity knocks they can answer. It's like the parable of the ten virgins in the New Testament—those who were full and ready stepped into the opportunity, those who didn' have their lamps full of oil and wicks trimmed missed it. We need to be ready for opportunity and position ourselves for success. If we prepare for success in the right way it's only a matter of time until opportunity will present itself. The local church needs to stop milking those in success for their money and tap into something of far greater value, wisdom! Just like in Solomon's day, when you get the wisdom, wealth and success come with it.

The local church should be an environment to facilitate success. This means equipping the saints for the work of the ministry beyond the pulpit or worship team; it means equipping them for life. We need to help them see how they can use their natural and spiritual gifts to succeed, build God's kingdom and use their influence and success to pastor our city. This is how we create the path of the least resistance so the wave of God can flow into, through and out from the local church.

This creates a move of God in our city that is sustainable, measurable and transferrable.

The local church has a mantle of authority on it for the spiritual realm.

> *For we do not wrestle against flesh and blood, but against principalities, against powers, against the rulers of the darkness of this age, against spiritual hosts of wickedness in the heavenly places.*
>
> *Ephesians 6:12*

We are called to deal with the spiritual realm using the principles I have presented earlier, which establishes a new authority in the heavenlies and creates an open heaven over our city. This authority is given as the local church takes the responsibility before God for the well being of their city. Those who take responsibility are given the authority. When the church has done it's job, the marketplace can tap into an open heaven and the spiritual authority they need to deal with any demonic force that would try to limit their success. This is where the signs and wonders are seen. We don't need to wait until the people come to the church—through the marketplace we can take the church to them!

Role of the marketplace in transformation

I think the local church should start by apologizing to the marketplace leaders for treating them like cash cows instead of embracing the wisdom that made them successful in the first place. We also need to invite them into the vision of city transformation, listen to their wisdom and tap into their anointing and influence. Just as the local church has authority for the spiritual realm I believe the marketplace has the gift of influence. We need both to pastor a city. Authority is for the spiritual realms. When we deal with people we need great influence.

Wealth, character, integrity and a heart for the city increases your influence. The higher the levels of success or the more wealth you have acquired the more influence you have in your city. Even those who lack character but have wealth have a greater influence than those who have character but no success. We need the influence that comes from success on board with pastoring our city or we may gain spiritual authority in the heavenlies but lack the influence to bring it into a tangible reality in the natural.

The moral well being of our city and the direction it takes in the future isn't controlled by the ministerial; the influence is in the marketplace. Issues of society like bars and strip clubs, vlt's or gambling casinos aren't controlled by the local churches. Anyone who wants to establish an entity of this nature would already have taken into consideration the opposition of the local church. We may have authority to deal with the spirit realm but right now we need a strong voice of influence in the natural. Ten churches can rise up in opposition and be ignored. But when ten people or ten successful businesses of wealth and influence speak out, the issue is on the front page of the news. We need this kind of influence working with us to successfully pastor our city. With this ability or influence in our cities comes a responsibility. The direction and nature of the development of our city is in the hands of the marketplace. What they want they will get. The church can say no, but if the marketplace leaders of wealth and influence say yes, they will lead the community in the direction they choose to go. To pastor our city we need to have them on board with the God-given vision for our city. So it becomes our responsibility to gather them together, embrace their wisdom and allow them a major voice in turning prophetic revelation into an apostolic reality.

They are the ones who have the right gifting to develop a blueprint for city transformation. This blueprint outlines the role each sector takes and the responsibility it carries to lead the community into its purpose.

They also have the privilege of lobbying political leaders. We tend to think politicians don't like lobbyists, but in actual fact they embrace feedback from the marketplace. It helps to determine the key issues and get a sense of the desires of the people. Also, elected officials are like most pastors, we aren't the most qualified people to deal with the issues of society, we are only trying to represent those who are. It creates an opportunity for Christian business leaders to have a voice in community development in infrastructure, economic development and social policy.

They are the ones who need to shoulder the vision of the community because they are the ones with the wealth and influence to turn the prophetic revelations into an apostolic reality. The marketplace also has the opportunity to create environments to mentor the next generation. It takes the support of the marketplace to sustain a generational vision.

Where we go wrong most times in the body of Christ is when the marketplace goes on their own without the local church. Although they can have some degrees of success in the salvation of souls or good deeds for the city, the spiritual climate, direction or nature of the city generally (not always) remains the same. After the movement passes by, everything reverts back to it''s former state until another wave passes through. To have a generational transformation we need to change the spiritual climate and then cleanse the land.

I use an illustration about a man who has a hate for an ethnic group. We counsel him and find out that in his teen years he was dragged out back and beat half to death by a gang of this particular people group. We can give Christian council, return to the violation and lead him into forgiveness. This can bring healing to the event itself, but if the attitudes and actions that were created after the violation don't change the stronghold still has power even if the event has been healed. We need to deal with the root issues of our lives but we also need to break off the attitudes and actions that came after the event. If we don't, the devil can use the attitudes and actions even though the event in itself is gone and dealt with.

On a citywide scale we need to deal with root issues. When we do it gives us jurisdictional authority. The authority is used to cleanse the land. We need the influence of the marketplace ministries to cleanse the attitudes and actions from our cities. They can function in an opposite spirit and create values-based companies as they build core values and character into their employees. These companies make the individual and their family just as important as profit. We also go wrong when the church tries to go out into the community by itself without the influence of the marketplace. We may have the authority in the spiritual realms to be out there but we still lack impact. This happens because we don't have the influence to mobilize them in the direction we want to go or to accept the values we want to establish.

When we partner the two entities of church and marketplace we are layering the anointings and increasing our impact and we get the best of both worlds. The marketplace then has access to the authority they need to deal with devils. The church then has the influence it needs to reach man.

This is how we are leading our city. We aren't serving man or an organization—we are serving the will or redemptive purpose of God for our city. As we pastor our city's redemptive purpose, the church grows as a by-product and the marketplace gets breakthroughs to abundance.

When we allow people to just be good at being who God has created them to be, embrace their gift and calling and partner them all together in an Acts 1 unity, fellowship and one accord, heaven bows down and touches earth, the gospel is preached, the city is pastored and God is glorified.

The marketplace has the task of possessing the land, being ambassadors for Jesus to the community, making lots of money to break the poverty spirit of the kingdom of God and to win the world to Jesus. They are the ones who do the work of the ministry. The ministry done in the church or "boot camp" is to equip them to be good at being who God has called and gifted them to be and to create environments of relationship and service to the Lord.

The role of the intercessor

If you take the time to think through the idea of the ARC network described earlier you will get some ideas of structure. Now I would like to talk about their role in transformation.

I start with the premise that intercession is a valued gift but not an authoritive or office ministry. It has authority only when it's under authority.

This is a key issue if we want to bring prophetic revelation into an apostolic reality. Intercessors are great gifted people and need to be recognized and honored in the body of Christ. Just think about it for a moment. There are those in the body who are passionate about nothing else but prayer! Jesus said "My house shall be called a house of prayer."

They are valued and are very important in both dimensions of getting the prophetic revelations and making the apostolic proclamations. We have many different types of intercessory prayer teams in our church.

1. SWAT or our Spiritual Warfare Apostolic Team. This team presses into the Lord for revelations and fights the spiritual strongholds when asked. They also do the historic research to confirm the revelations. This is about seventy-five percent of their time. They partner with the vision and timing of the pastor and exercise the authority of the church into the spiritual realm when given the instruction.

2. Mountain Movers. This team prays for the issues of society. Sometimes they take the issues from the local paper and bring them before the Lord. At other times they are making apostolic proclamations about the will of the Lord for the city. These proclamations don't come by inspiration, they come by permission and instruction of the apostolic leadership team. They don't chase the darkness, they proclaim the light. But now they have the authority and the gifts working to proclaim it.

3. Family Prayer Team. This group prays through the issues of an individual or family received by request on prayer cards using the formula "Prophetic revelation, confirmed by natural knowledge and released by permission."

4. Marketplace prayer. This team partners and prays

for the marketplace ministries. They cover issues of protection, wisdom, strategies and any direct request from the marketplace leaders themselves. Our goal is to have every marketplace ministry covered by a personal prayer shield and intercessory team.

5. Youth prayer. This is a prayer team that makes the proclamations into their generation.

6. Prayer shields. Every team leader must have a prayer shield. Their role is to pray that our faith won't fail.

7. Healing prayer. These teams work with individuals to deal with the root issues of their souls. They ask the Lord to expose the lies we have allowed into our lives and to replace them with a word of truth.

8. Altar prayer. These teams pray for the people after the services.

All intercession needs to be judged. Prophetic people are gifted at revelation but not necessarily good at timing or strategic implementation. The revelations need to be judged by the apostolic team government that watches over them. This means an intercessor must be willing to submit their ministry to the guidance of the authority of the local church leadership. This isn't control, it's a strength and a protection—a strength because they have authority when they are under authority. It also protects them from chasing after darkness, getting hurt or getting way out into bad doctrinal principles. If they work independently of the local church they can actually be functioning in witchcraft.

All revelations need to be judged in the following categories. Given the assumption that the revelation is first scripturally sound, it still needs to be judged for dimension and timing. Is the word revealing issues of the past we need to deal with? Is it revealing issues of the present we need to address now or issues of the future to indicate warnings or blessings of the Lord?

Revelations also need to be judged to determine the target group they are for. The revelation may be for the individual. Many times intercessors get a word from the Lord they should apply to their own life and they try to put it on the church. Is it for the individual, the church or the city? Many pastors get words for their own ministry or their own church and try to put it on the city.

The point is this. We all need people in our lives whose judgements we trust beyond our personal revelations. We see Peter's revelations in Matthew 16. Peter got revelation from the Father the first time and from the devil the second and he couldn't tell the difference. We won't be able to tell, either.

We need the revelations to be judged by people we trust beyond our personal revelations. If we don't have them built into our system it's only a matter of time until we run into problems.

Intercessors work with the leadership team to get revelations. They do the historical research to confirm the revelations with natural knowledge. Then they help and give input for strategies and help the governing team to judge the revelations and develop the strategies. Then they, under authority and by permission, make apostolic proclamations.

The proclamations are proclaimed over our city or nation. This is apostolic prayer. Declare a thing (while under authority) and it will be established for you.

In our eleven years of spiritual warfare and city

transformation we have never had any problems with our intercessory prayer teams. This is due to two keys: 1) we have a prayer pastor that trains, equips and watches over all the prayer initiatives, and 2) the SWAT, marketplace and family prayer teams aren't open to drop-in crowds. These team members are mentored, trained and approved before they are allowed to attend any meetings. This gives the history, skills and team co-operation principles to do safe and effective intercession. We aren't here to chase the darkness but to turn on the lights!

Summary of the process of city transformation:

1. Identify your weakness and your strengths.

2. Know your personal redemptive purpose.

3. Determine your church's redemptive purpose.

4. Study the history of the region (do spiritual mapping) so you can confirm revelations with natural knowledge.

5. Build prayer teams in your church and in your city.

6. Determine and define the nature of your city today.

    a. When in history was it on track with Gods' purpose?

    b. When did it change?

    c. What happened? What decisions were made that appeared right in the natural but violated the purposes of God? Who made them?

7. Do identificational repentance. Go before God and repent of the errors of your forefathers and ask Him to show you and help you to redeem the city back into its purpose. (This closes the doorway and removes the legal rights for the demonic force to be there.)

8. Repent before God for the violations or sins that came as a result of the error (cleanse the land).

9. Connect with other churches and their redemptive purpose.

10. Connect all churches as a team to the city's purpose.

11. Develop a long-term city strategy.

12. Send info to a regional Facilitator or the prayer centre to get more prayer in action!

Summary: The Four strongholds

The four main powers or spirits I believe we are dealing with in the spirit realm are:

1. The spirit or **_attitude of error_** - Headship violation of making decisions with what seems right to the carnal man instead of being obedient to the instructions and purposes of God.

2. The **_spirit of Leviathan_** - controlling principality partnering with James 3:16 leadership.

3. The **_spirit of strife_** that works in the people and robs the harvest.

4. The **_spirit of rebellion_** that works like witchcraft – God's people that use their position, abilities and influence for personal gain against the purposes of God and His people.

The 3 principles needed to bring transformation to your city.

I. Jurisdictional authority
Involving:
1. The Redemptive Purposes of God
2. Personal Spiritual Authority
3. Corporate anointing - train a leader, build a team, to accomplish a task

II. Servanthood to the redemptive purpose
Involving:
1. Humility - acts of humility brings true spiritual authority
2. Integrity - finding and restoring "the original state of a thing" or the redemptive purpose
3. Maturity - Obedience to His leading

III-Vehicles of influence
Involving:
1. 1-Administration - "to lead by serving and to serve by administration"
2. Character - expressions of love to the community
3. Relationship - windows and doors of communication

If you use the principles contained in this testimonial book, you will increase your **"Power to Effect Change!"**

My Final Thoughts

There are three principles needed to bring transformation to your city

1. **The Jurisdictional authority of the local church into the heavenlies**

2. **Servanthood to the Redemptive Purpose of the city**

3. **Marketplace vehicles of influence**

While traveling and listening to what the body of Christ is being led into, I can see a common strategic thread. The basic mindset is the saturation and infiltration of our cities. We are having great successes with this strategy. Many are finding the need of their city and stepping up to the plate to meet that need. This is good for us to do and I say good for every effort and every work that's being done in the name of the Lord.

As a city councilor I attend many conferences about city development or social programming. At one of these meetings we were taught a principle that I thought brought a strategic revelation for the body of Christ. We were taught about municipal budgets. Our budgets never seem to overcome our needs. We have more infrastructure needs than the tax base will support. We know that over time we have a good chance of recovering the investment, but how do you get the up front capital needed? This is a question all municipalities are addressing, at least in our province.

With limited resources and great need we start to prioritize our projects and focus our attention on the greatest needs first. Let me use roads as an example. We don't have the resources to build or to maintain all the roads we need at once so we have to prioritize our projects and logic leads us to the worst roads first. This is logical, but it creates a long-term perpetual problem. If we put our limited resources to work and focus our attention on a repairing the bad road program and don't put at least equal attention and resources to building and maintaining the good roads, eventually all good roads become bad ones. This focus of resources and manpower creates a continual bad road maintenance program.

When this was taught it gripped my spirit as a parallel of what the body of Christ has become, a perpetual repairing of broken roads or caring for those who aren't able to care for themselves.

Don't get me wrong, this needs to be done, but we need to balance the strategy with an aggressive action plan to build the new roads and maintain the ones already in use. Even in the local church we hear about twenty percent of the people getting eighty percent of our time. If the twenty percent are the ones in distress, indebted and discouraged and we focus most of our time and resources addressing the problem, who is maintaining and building the ministries that just need to be mentored to a higher level of success? If the strong and able people of the church are left alone because our time, our programs and our resources are only used to help those in need, eventually all good roads will get beaten up and in need of repair and we will develop a perpetual broken road, maintenance culture in our church. This attracts more broken roads and can even grow a church. This strategy can even make a difference in our city but in itself it won't bring sustainable transformation.

We are constantly looking for the need of the city and opportunity to infiltrate culture with the gospel. We try to get Christians involved in city hall, education or sports and work on strategies of saturation of society.

Here in Drayton we took the eighty percent principle and turned it around. If twenty percent were going to use up eighty percent of our time we decided to identify the top twenty percent fruitful ministry people in our church and pour a large portion of our time, resources and energy into them. Through their success and abilities, and even with limited resources we were able to help more people in need than with a "repairing the broken road" strategy.

There are churches that have a Redemptive Purpose to help the needy with soup kitchens and shelters. I also realize the instructions of scripture to us all to care for those in need, so I'm not suggesting we shouldn't do it. It's how we pastor our city that I'm suggesting. There are some churches that are gifted and strong dealing directly with the needy. But some are strong in developing business leaders, politicians or some in education. If we can't do it all as an individual church, we should work together in a corporate team dynamic in our city to repair the broken roads AND build and maintain the new ones.

Our church started to put most of our attention on leadership training. Now we have strong people, effective ministries and loyal people to help repair the "broken roads" of our city. We took this principle and applied it to our city strategy as well. We have built relationships with those who have the wealth and influence to make a difference. One successful businessperson with a heart of compassion for the needy can make more of a financial impact than a half-dozen churches doing fundraisers for a year. When we adopted this action plan we gained credibility with the city through not coming with our hands out wanting something, but rather, coming with our hands reaching out giving something back to the community. The walls came down, the trust was established, the doors of the city swung open and the church was embraced. This allowed us into every sector of our city, not by saturation or infiltration but by invitation! We have partnered with the city leaders, successful businesses and education systems to address the needs or the people.

This has increased our profile, established our credibility and increased our impact.

In order to do this you need community alignment or the defined direction and purpose your city is trying to go. Many times a church will be trying to lead their city without knowing where it is wanting to go. This strategy without defined direction forces us to follow the city, picking up those who can't make it on their own or who have fallen along the way. Again, please don't get me wrong, this, too, needs to be done! My point is, if you want to lead you have to be out in front. We are to be the head and not the tail. So we have a two-fold purpose, to lead and to meet the need. If we focus on one and not the other we may have successes but not transformation.

To lead a community we need to know where God wants it to go. We get this through prophetic revelation and historical research.

The "find the need" saturation strategies have an apostolic or strategic nature to them and bear much fruit for the glory of God. But history shows these strategies help many people but don't create sustainable, measurable and transferable transformation of cities and nations in themselves.

I put it this way. An apostolic strategy without the prophetic revelation will bring saturation but not transformation. This is due to the unchanged spiritual realms over the city or nation.

Our goal is to bring prophetic revelation into an apostolic reality. This takes building on the foundation of the apostles AND the prophets. We need to get the revelations, confirm them with natural knowledge or research of the history of our city and then take this revelation through an apostolic or leadership team to be judged for accuracy, developed into strategy and put under authority. Then the strategies can be released to prayer teams. The job of the prayer ministry now isn't to fight the darkness or get the revelations, that's already done. (As taught earlier, by the time you can name the strongholds you are fighting you have already won them). The task now is to proclaim the will and strategy of God over the city. This establishes the principles and the authority in the heavens.

Under the authority in the heavenlies the mind of the marketplace starts to shift to God's thoughts and God's plans. Businesses that co-operate with the plans of God prosper and grow, those who don't struggle. This is the dividing line of blessing, not just being born-again. You can be born-again and rebel against the plans of God and struggle, or you can be totally unchurched but heading the right way or in the direction God wants the city to go and tap into the blessing of God. The blessing of God shines upon the just and the unjust, the righteous or unrighteous equally.

There is a possibility that the words "the wealth of the nation is stored up for the righteous" means "all those who are doing what is right or heading in the direction God wants the city to go will find increase and blessing." I do believe there is a special blessing for God's people in this, but I do see a principle of blessing that crosses the boundaries of church. Maybe many have succeeded in our city because they have tapped into the right principles to move our city where God wants it to go. If the church doesn't lead the city, God can use totally unchurched people. We see it in the Bible. God used heathen nations to do His will when His people wouldn't co-operate. The point is, we may be able to learn something about the direction and will of God for our city by analyzing the marketplace dynamics.

The God-strength of our city may be right there in front of us to see. The gifts and nature of commerce may be a sign of the Redemptive Purpose giftings of God on the city. Take a look and see what you find!

One day the mantle of authority and the grace of the message will be re-united! As the Apostolic ministry is established in the body of Christ there will once again be a movement to establish "kingdom government." There will come a day when the body of Christ will have kingdom authority with a gospel of grace!

The term "Apostle" has caused much debate in every organization around the world. I believe this is only the beginning. There will come a time when a one world spiritual government will be established in a good and Godly way. In every church we have someone who is recognized as a senior elder or Pastor. Every organization has someone who would be generally acknowledged as the senior elder or Apostle, or leader. The structure will continue into the national realms of inter-faith government. There will come a time when there will be senior leaders from many faiths (born-again) who will form what I see as an international Jerusalem council that will give oversight to national councils that give oversight to regions, etc.

The function of this council isn't to dictate to the body of Christ, but to do what the Jerusalem council did. Among their many functions they...

> 1. Affirmed ministries. They gave the Apostle Paul the right hand of fellowship.

2. They set guidelines "when asked." The guidelines in the letters they wrote to establish the new churches are still used today.

3. They were agents of change. They helped others make the transition from Old Testament laws, theology and traditions to the Gospel of grace.

There are many other reasons for their existence, but the point is that there will one day be a return of this consensus style of government to the International church of Jesus Christ! Government shall be on His shoulders! The body of Christ starts with government!

This will be a "kingdom government" with a "gospel message." It will be grace with power!

Then we will truly have...

"The Power to Effect Change!"

This establishes a new spiritual climate over a city... where, **"the people of a region can surrender to God's influence on their carnal nature that will develop mental attitudes driven by Godly forces!"**

In the early years of our church the Lord spoke to us and said there would be two winds coming our way. Only those who would turn into the first wind would be propelled forward by the second one. The first wind brought a cleansing and those who turned into it, went through a season of cleansing that was intense. Those who turned away from it left our community.

Then we hit a season of stillness. The Lord showed us it was like the eye of a hurricane that we were in and that the wind would come again, only this time it would be from the other way.

As the cleansing wind blowing towards us stopped, the stillness was a safe place while waiting for the wind to change direction and begin propelling us forward! The wind started again and it has been blowing us forward ever since.

This book isn't intended to change the way you believe. My intent was to stir some thoughts and bring some fresh inspiration to you, with possibly some new ideas to help you. It is a testimony of what we have lived.

I hope it has helped.
Gary W. Carter

Training Seminars Available

The Power to Effect Change!

This training seminar covers the principles of this book. It is designed to mobilize the body of Christ to transform cities and nations. 6 hours.

Human Factor

This course was developed by Bill Galston. In the times we live in technology has advanced to near perfection. The main cause of incident now isn't usually faulty equipment but human error. We cover communication, stress, assertive leadership, dealing with conflict and other human issues of the workplace. This can be used for secular leadership training as well as local church. 6 hours.

Marketing non-tangible products

We know how to sell a car or any other item but how do you market non-tangible products like integrity, character or the gospel etc. This seminar has workshop elements that helps to define your target audience, purpose and growth strategies. Good for secular audiences as well. 6 hours.

Leadership training

This covers many topics and can even be custom designed for your need. We cover corporate team dynamics, self motivated leadership, self-correcting leadership, the qualities of a leader, profiling potential and many other leadership issues. 6 to 12 hours.

Character training

This program is designed as a character building tool to help to implement core values into your leadership training, employee development, family strength, business ethic or city image. 6 hours.

Prayer in the local church

This three-hour training course is led by our prayer pastor and her team. It covers the principles we have developed in our churches over the last ten years to have safe and effective prayer teams. It covers the vital role of the pastors, the guidelines for the intercessor and how to partner the gift with the authority of the local church. It covers our Spiritual warfare team, mountain movers, prayer walking your city, prayer shields, youth prayer, family prayer principles, marketplace prayer teams, altar prayer and many other creative and effective principles to strengthen the local church and transform your city or nation.

These are only a few of the courses we offer in our Leadership Training Centre. Many other courses are offered on request. Contact us at 1-780-621-0277 or at www.dvwordoflife.com

9 781894 928021